TEACHER'S PET PUBLICATIONS

PUZZLE PACK
for
Tangerine

based on the book by
Edward Bloor

Written by
Mary B. Collins

© 2008 Teacher's Pet Publications
All Rights Reserved

The materials in this packet are copyrighted
by Teacher's Pet Publications, Inc.

These pages may be duplicated by the purchaser
for use in the purchaser's own classroom.

Copying any of these materials and distributing them
for any other purpose is a violation of the copyright laws.

© 2008 Teacher's Pet Publications, Inc.
www.tpet.com

INTRODUCTION
If you already own the LitPlan for this title, this Puzzle Pack will refresh your Unit Resource Materials and Vocabulary Resource Materials sections plus give you additional materials you can substitute into the tests. If you do not already have a complete LitPlan, these pages will give you some supplemental materials to use with your own plan. There are two main groups of materials: one set for unit words (such as characters' names, symbols, places, etc.) and one set for vocabulary words associated with the book.

WORD LIST
There is a word list for both the unit words and the vocabulary words. These lists show you which words are being used in the materials and the clues or definitions being used for those words. You may want to give students a word list with clues/definitions to help them, or you may want students to only have a word list (without clues/definitions) if you want them to work a little harder. Both are available for duplication. The word lists can also be your "calling key" for the bingo games.

FILL IN THE BLANK AND MATCHING
There are 4 each of the fill in the blank and matching worksheets for both the unit and vocabulary words. These pages can be used either as extra worksheets for students or as objective parts of a unit test. They can be done individually if students need extra help or as a whole class activity to review the material covered.

MAGIC SQUARES
The magic squares not only reinforce the material covered but also work on reasoning and math skills. Many teachers have told us that their students really enjoy doing these!

WORD SEARCH PUZZLES
The word search words go in all directions, as indicated on your answer keys. Two of the word search puzzles have the clues listed rather than the words. This makes the puzzle a little more difficult, but it reinforces the material better. Two word search puzzles have words only for students who find the clue puzzles too difficult.

CROSSWORD PUZZLES
Both unit and vocabulary word sections have 4 crossword puzzles.

BINGO CARDS
There are 32 individual bingo cards for the unit words and 32 individual bingo cards for the vocabulary words. You can use your word list as a "call list," calling the words at random and marking them off of your list as you go, or you could use the flash cards by cutting them apart and drawing the words at random from a hat (or box or whatever). To make a better review, you might ask for the definition and spelling of each word as you call it out–or you could call out the definitions and have students tell you the words they need to look for on the puzzle.

JUGGLE LETTERS
The vocabulary juggle letter game is intended to help students learn the spellings of the words. One sheet has the definitions listed on it as an extra help for students who need it or to reinforce the definitions if you choose to do so.

FLASH CARDS
We've included a set of vocabulary flash cards you can duplicate, cut, and fold for your students. Some teachers make a few sets for general use by the class; others make a set for each student. Some teachers duplicate them for each student and have the students cut & fold their own. You can cut out just the words and put them in a hat, have each student pick out one word and write the definition and a sentence for that word. Students then swap words and papers, with the next student adding a sentence of his own under the last one. You can have students swap as many times as you like. Each time the student will read the sentences written prior to his own and then add a sentence. You can cut out the words and definitions separately and play "I Have; Who Has?" Each student in the room draws a word and definition. The first student says, "I have (the name of the word). Who has the definition?" The student with the definition reads it then says, "I have (the name of the vocabulary word she has). Who has the definition?" The round continues until all words and definitions have been given.

Tangerine Word List

No.	Word	Clue/Definition
1.	ANEURYSM	Cause of Luis's death
2.	ANTOINE	Person who pulls the ball away from Erik as he goes to kick for a last minute play
3.	ARTHUR	Erik's sidekick
4.	AWARD	Tino and Victor go to the ___ ceremony to get revenge on Erik.
5.	BLACKJACK	Arthur uses it to hit Luis.
6.	BRIGHT	Coach who participated in the Olympics for track and field
7.	BROTHER	Tino calls Paul this, letting him know everything is good in their friendship.
8.	BUS	Being on the ___ at Lake Windsor means you get to play the away games.
9.	CARNIVAL	Paul rats out the Tangerine soccer players for vandalizing an exhibit at the ___.
10.	DAWN	Luis creates a tangerine called the Golden ___.
11.	ECLIPSE	Paul tells people he looked at an ___ for too long, causing damage to his eyes.
12.	EXPELLED	Paul gets ___ from school for his actions at the award ceremony.
13.	FISHER	Paul's nickname at Tangerine
14.	FLASHBACKS	Paul occasionally has these, about the past.
15.	FLORIDA	State where Paul and his family move to at the start of the novel
16.	FOOTBALL	The Erik Fisher ___ Dream
17.	FREEZE	Paul helps the Cruz family care for their tangerines during the ___.
18.	FUNERAL	Paul is asked not to attend Luis's.
19.	GIRLS	Paul and his mom are shocked to see THEY play on the soccer team.
20.	GOALIE	Position on the soccer team Paul has always played in the past
21.	GOGGLES	Paul wears these on his eyes while playing soccer.
22.	GRANDPARENTS	Paul's are not interested in Erik's football achievements and plans.
23.	HENRY	Theresa, Tino, and ___ all work with Paul on a school project.
24.	HEROES	Paul and Joey act as ___ during the sinkhole disaster.
25.	HOUSTON	Former home of the Fisher family
26.	IEP	Prevents Paul from playing soccer at LWD; later "disappears"
27.	JOEY	Transfers to Tangerine Middle School and hates it
28.	KERRI	Girl who likes Paul
29.	LIGHTNING	Kills Mike Castello
30.	MARS	Paul's nickname at Lake Windsor
31.	MORNING	Paul's mom wants practice moved to this time of day.
32.	MOSQUITOS	Side effect of soaking the fields in water to get rid of the fires
33.	MUCK	This type of fire is continuously burning behind Paul's house.
34.	MUD	Someone smears this in Paul's face, causing him to start a fight.
35.	NULLIFIES	The county ___ all LW victories in which Antoine played.
36.	OSPREYS	Cause the coy in the pond to disappear
37.	PAUL	His older brother gets all the attention of his parents.
38.	POLICE	Paul prepares a statement for the ___ explaining what he

		witnessed.
39.	PUNCH	Paul thinks his dad saw Erik ___ Tino, but he did nothing.
40.	RELIEVED	How Paul says he would feel if his brother died
41.	SCHOLARSHIP	Paul finds a file on his dad's computer about Erik's ___ offers.
42.	SHANDRA	Antoine's little sister who plays on Paul's soccer team
43.	SHOES	Joey tries to take these off of his brother.
44.	SINKHOLE	Does severe damage to Lake Windsor Middle School
45.	SOCCER	Paul's sport
46.	STORAGE	Paul's mom finds the stolen goods in the ___ unit.
47.	TERMITES	The houses tented for ___ were being robbed.
48.	THERESA	Shows Paul around school on the first day
49.	TINO	Starts a fight with Joey over a comment he made about Luis
50.	TREE	Luis hurts his leg permanently from falling out of one.
51.	WAR	Tangerine's teams are known as the ___ Eagles.

Tangerine Fill In The Blanks 1

1. Tangerine's teams are known as the ___ Eagles.
2. Erik's sidekick
3. Paul's mom wants practice moved to this time of day.
4. State where Paul and his family move to at the start of the novel
5. Coach who participated in the Olympics for track and field
6. Shows Paul around school on the first day
7. Arthur uses it to hit Luis.
8. Paul rats out the Tangerine soccer players for vandalizing an exhibit at the ___.
9. Cause of Luis's death
10. Cause the coy in the pond to disappear
11. Being on the ___ at Lake Windsor means you get to play the away games.
12. Girl who likes Paul
13. Joey tries to take these off of his brother.
14. Kills Mike Castello
15. Paul helps the Cruz family care for their tangerines during the ___.
16. How Paul says he would feel if his brother died
17. Former home of the Fisher family
18. Theresa, Tino, and ___ all work with Paul on a school project.
19. Side effect of soaking the fields in water to get rid of the fires
20. Paul's nickname at Lake Windsor

Tangerine Fill In The Blanks 1 Answer Key

WAR	1. Tangerine's teams are known as the ___ Eagles.
ARTHUR	2. Erik's sidekick
MORNING	3. Paul's mom wants practice moved to this time of day.
FLORIDA	4. State where Paul and his family move to at the start of the novel
BRIGHT	5. Coach who participated in the Olympics for track and field
THERESA	6. Shows Paul around school on the first day
BLACKJACK	7. Arthur uses it to hit Luis.
CARNIVAL	8. Paul rats out the Tangerine soccer players for vandalizing an exhibit at the ___.
ANEURYSM	9. Cause of Luis's death
OSPREYS	10. Cause the coy in the pond to disappear
BUS	11. Being on the ___ at Lake Windsor means you get to play the away games.
KERRI	12. Girl who likes Paul
SHOES	13. Joey tries to take these off of his brother.
LIGHTNING	14. Kills Mike Castello
FREEZE	15. Paul helps the Cruz family care for their tangerines during the ___.
RELIEVED	16. How Paul says he would feel if his brother died
HOUSTON	17. Former home of the Fisher family
HENRY	18. Theresa, Tino, and ___ all work with Paul on a school project.
MOSQUITOS	19. Side effect of soaking the fields in water to get rid of the fires
MARS	20. Paul's nickname at Lake Windsor

Tangerine Fill In The Blanks 2

_____

_____

_____

_____

_____

_____

_____

_____

_____

_____

_____

_____

_____

_____

_____

_____

_____

_____

_____

_____

1. How Paul says he would feel if his brother died
2. Someone smears this in Paul's face, causing him to start a fight.
3. Theresa, Tino, and ___ all work with Paul on a school project.
4. Luis hurts his leg permanently from falling out of one.
5. Paul's nickname at Tangerine
6. Starts a fight with Joey over a comment he made about Luis
7. Arthur uses it to hit Luis.
8. Luis creates a tangerine called the Golden ___.
9. His older brother gets all the attention of his parents.
10. Joey tries to take these off of his brother.
11. Being on the ___ at Lake Windsor means you get to play the away games.
12. Former home of the Fisher family
13. Kills Mike Castello
14. Paul and his mom are shocked to see THEY play on the soccer team.
15. Side effect of soaking the fields in water to get rid of the fires
16. Paul's are not interested in Erik's football achievements and plans.
17. Paul prepares a statement for the ___ explaining what he witnessed.
18. Shows Paul around school on the first day
19. Paul finds a file on his dad's computer about Erik's ___ offers.
20. Tangerine's teams are known as the ___ Eagles.

Tangerine Fill In The Blanks 2 Answer Key

RELIEVED	1. How Paul says he would feel if his brother died
MUD	2. Someone smears this in Paul's face, causing him to start a fight.
HENRY	3. Theresa, Tino, and ___ all work with Paul on a school project.
TREE	4. Luis hurts his leg permanently from falling out of one.
FISHER	5. Paul's nickname at Tangerine
TINO	6. Starts a fight with Joey over a comment he made about Luis
BLACKJACK	7. Arthur uses it to hit Luis.
DAWN	8. Luis creates a tangerine called the Golden ___.
PAUL	9. His older brother gets all the attention of his parents.
SHOES	10. Joey tries to take these off of his brother.
BUS	11. Being on the ___ at Lake Windsor means you get to play the away games.
HOUSTON	12. Former home of the Fisher family
LIGHTNING	13. Kills Mike Castello
GIRLS	14. Paul and his mom are shocked to see THEY play on the soccer team.
MOSQUITOS	15. Side effect of soaking the fields in water to get rid of the fires
GRANDPARENTS	16. Paul's are not interested in Erik's football achievements and plans.
POLICE	17. Paul prepares a statement for the ___ explaining what he witnessed.
THERESA	18. Shows Paul around school on the first day
SCHOLARSHIP	19. Paul finds a file on his dad's computer about Erik's ___ offers.
WAR	20. Tangerine's teams are known as the ___ Eagles.

Tangerine Fill In The Blanks 3

_____
_____
_____
_____
_____
_____
_____
_____
_____
_____
_____
_____
_____
_____
_____
_____
_____
_____
_____
_____

1. Paul gets ___ from school for his actions at the award ceremony.
2. His older brother gets all the attention of his parents.
3. Paul's mom finds the stolen goods in the ___ unit.
4. Paul thinks his dad saw Erik ___ Tino, but he did nothing.
5. Paul's sport
6. Side effect of soaking the fields in water to get rid of the fires
7. The Erik Fisher ___ Dream
8. Transfers to Tangerine Middle School and hates it
9. Kills Mike Castello
10. Paul finds a file on his dad's computer about Erik's ___ offers.
11. Paul prepares a statement for the ___ explaining what he witnessed.
12. Paul rats out the Tangerine soccer players for vandalizing an exhibit at the ___.
13. Paul is asked not to attend Luis's.
14. Shows Paul around school on the first day
15. Former home of the Fisher family
16. The county ___ all LW victories in which Antoine played.
17. Does severe damage to Lake Windsor Middle School
18. Tangerine's teams are known as the ___ Eagles.
19. Joey tries to take these off of his brother.
20. Paul tells people he looked at an ___ for too long, causing damage to his eyes.

Tangerine Fill In The Blanks 3 Answer Key

EXPELLED	1. Paul gets ___ from school for his actions at the award ceremony.
PAUL	2. His older brother gets all the attention of his parents.
STORAGE	3. Paul's mom finds the stolen goods in the ___ unit.
PUNCH	4. Paul thinks his dad saw Erik ___ Tino, but he did nothing.
SOCCER	5. Paul's sport
MOSQUITOS	6. Side effect of soaking the fields in water to get rid of the fires
FOOTBALL	7. The Erik Fisher ___ Dream
JOEY	8. Transfers to Tangerine Middle School and hates it
LIGHTNING	9. Kills Mike Castello
SCHOLARSHIP	10. Paul finds a file on his dad's computer about Erik's ___ offers.
POLICE	11. Paul prepares a statement for the ___ explaining what he witnessed.
CARNIVAL	12. Paul rats out the Tangerine soccer players for vandalizing an exhibit at the ___.
FUNERAL	13. Paul is asked not to attend Luis's.
THERESA	14. Shows Paul around school on the first day
HOUSTON	15. Former home of the Fisher family
NULLIFIES	16. The county ___ all LW victories in which Antoine played.
SINKHOLE	17. Does severe damage to Lake Windsor Middle School
WAR	18. Tangerine's teams are known as the ___ Eagles.
SHOES	19. Joey tries to take these off of his brother.
ECLIPSE	20. Paul tells people he looked at an ___ for too long, causing damage to his eyes.

Tangerine Fill In The Blanks 4

1. Paul wears these on his eyes while playing soccer.
2. Side effect of soaking the fields in water to get rid of the fires
3. Someone smears this in Paul's face, causing him to start a fight.
4. Paul's nickname at Lake Windsor
5. Cause the coy in the pond to disappear
6. Paul's sport
7. Shows Paul around school on the first day
8. Position on the soccer team Paul has always played in the past
9. Tino and Victor go to the ___ ceremony to get revenge on Erik.
10. The houses tented for ___ were being robbed.
11. Joey tries to take these off of his brother.
12. Tangerine's teams are known as the ___ Eagles.
13. How Paul says he would feel if his brother died
14. Cause of Luis's death
15. Paul finds a file on his dad's computer about Erik's ___ offers.
16. Transfers to Tangerine Middle School and hates it
17. Paul and his mom are shocked to see THEY play on the soccer team.
18. Paul is asked not to attend Luis's.
19. Paul gets ___ from school for his actions at the award ceremony.
20. Erik's sidekick

Tangerine Fill In The Blanks 4 Answer Key

GOGGLES	1. Paul wears these on his eyes while playing soccer.
MOSQUITOS	2. Side effect of soaking the fields in water to get rid of the fires
MUD	3. Someone smears this in Paul's face, causing him to start a fight.
MARS	4. Paul's nickname at Lake Windsor
OSPREYS	5. Cause the coy in the pond to disappear
SOCCER	6. Paul's sport
THERESA	7. Shows Paul around school on the first day
GOALIE	8. Position on the soccer team Paul has always played in the past
AWARD	9. Tino and Victor go to the ___ ceremony to get revenge on Erik.
TERMITES	10. The houses tented for ___ were being robbed.
SHOES	11. Joey tries to take these off of his brother.
WAR	12. Tangerine's teams are known as the ___ Eagles.
RELIEVED	13. How Paul says he would feel if his brother died
ANEURYSM	14. Cause of Luis's death
SCHOLARSHIP	15. Paul finds a file on his dad's computer about Erik's ___ offers.
JOEY	16. Transfers to Tangerine Middle School and hates it
GIRLS	17. Paul and his mom are shocked to see THEY play on the soccer team.
FUNERAL	18. Paul is asked not to attend Luis's.
EXPELLED	19. Paul gets ___ from school for his actions at the award ceremony.
ARTHUR	20. Erik's sidekick

Tangerine Matching 1

___ 1. MARS
___ 2. GRANDPARENTS
___ 3. HEROES
___ 4. FLASHBACKS
___ 5. HENRY
___ 6. GOALIE
___ 7. MOSQUITOS
___ 8. JOEY
___ 9. SINKHOLE
___ 10. BLACKJACK
___ 11. CARNIVAL
___ 12. OSPREYS
___ 13. TREE
___ 14. FLORIDA
___ 15. TINO
___ 16. ANEURYSM
___ 17. KERRI
___ 18. PUNCH
___ 19. SHANDRA
___ 20. BRIGHT
___ 21. MUD
___ 22. FISHER
___ 23. GIRLS
___ 24. MUCK
___ 25. GOGGLES

A. Paul and his mom are shocked to see THEY play on the soccer team.
B. Does severe damage to Lake Windsor Middle School
C. Antoine's little sister who plays on Paul's soccer team
D. Coach who participated in the Olympics for track and field
E. Cause the coy in the pond to disappear
F. Cause of Luis's death
G. Paul rats out the Tangerine soccer players for vandalizing an exhibit at the ___.
H. Luis hurts his leg permanently from falling out of one.
I. Starts a fight with Joey over a comment he made about Luis
J. Paul's are not interested in Erik's football achievements and plans.
K. Arthur uses it to hit Luis.
L. Position on the soccer team Paul has always played in the past
M. Girl who likes Paul
N. Paul occasionally has these, about the past.
O. State where Paul and his family move to at the start of the novel
P. Paul's nickname at Lake Windsor
Q. Transfers to Tangerine Middle School and hates it
R. Side effect of soaking the fields in water to get rid of the fires
S. Paul and Joey act as ___ during the sinkhole disaster.
T. Someone smears this in Paul's face, causing him to start a fight.
U. This type of fire is continuously burning behind Paul's house.
V. Paul's nickname at Tangerine
W. Theresa, Tino, and ___ all work with Paul on a school project.
X. Paul wears these on his eyes while playing soccer.
Y. Paul thinks his dad saw Erik ___ Tino, but he did nothing.

Tangerine Matching 1 Answer Key

P - 1. MARS
J - 2. GRANDPARENTS
S - 3. HEROES
N - 4. FLASHBACKS
W - 5. HENRY
L - 6. GOALIE
R - 7. MOSQUITOS
Q - 8. JOEY
B - 9. SINKHOLE
K -10. BLACKJACK
G -11. CARNIVAL
E -12. OSPREYS
H -13. TREE
O -14. FLORIDA
I - 15. TINO
F -16. ANEURYSM
M -17. KERRI
Y -18. PUNCH
C -19. SHANDRA
D -20. BRIGHT
T -21. MUD
V -22. FISHER
A -23. GIRLS
U -24. MUCK
X -25. GOGGLES

A. Paul and his mom are shocked to see THEY play on the soccer team.
B. Does severe damage to Lake Windsor Middle School
C. Antoine's little sister who plays on Paul's soccer team
D. Coach who participated in the Olympics for track and field
E. Cause the coy in the pond to disappear
F. Cause of Luis's death
G. Paul rats out the Tangerine soccer players for vandalizing an exhibit at the ___.
H. Luis hurts his leg permanently from falling out of one.
I. Starts a fight with Joey over a comment he made about Luis
J. Paul's are not interested in Erik's football achievements and plans.
K. Arthur uses it to hit Luis.
L. Position on the soccer team Paul has always played in the past
M. Girl who likes Paul
N. Paul occasionally has these, about the past.
O. State where Paul and his family move to at the start of the novel
P. Paul's nickname at Lake Windsor
Q. Transfers to Tangerine Middle School and hates it
R. Side effect of soaking the fields in water to get rid of the fires
S. Paul and Joey act as ___ during the sinkhole disaster.
T. Someone smears this in Paul's face, causing him to start a fight.
U. This type of fire is continuously burning behind Paul's house.
V. Paul's nickname at Tangerine
W. Theresa, Tino, and ___ all work with Paul on a school project.
X. Paul wears these on his eyes while playing soccer.
Y. Paul thinks his dad saw Erik ___ Tino, but he did nothing.

Tangerine Matching 2

___ 1. STORAGE
___ 2. WAR
___ 3. SOCCER
___ 4. HEROES
___ 5. MUD
___ 6. MORNING
___ 7. FLORIDA
___ 8. GOALIE
___ 9. BROTHER
___ 10. PAUL
___ 11. ANEURYSM
___ 12. FREEZE
___ 13. FOOTBALL
___ 14. GIRLS
___ 15. SINKHOLE
___ 16. AWARD
___ 17. THERESA
___ 18. TERMITES
___ 19. SHANDRA
___ 20. BRIGHT
___ 21. POLICE
___ 22. SCHOLARSHIP
___ 23. IEP
___ 24. GRANDPARENTS
___ 25. FUNERAL

A. Paul helps the Cruz family care for their tangerines during the ___.
B. Shows Paul around school on the first day
C. Antoine's little sister who plays on Paul's soccer team
D. Paul's mom finds the stolen goods in the ___ unit.
E. Coach who participated in the Olympics for track and field
F. Cause of Luis's death
G. Does severe damage to Lake Windsor Middle School
H. Tangerine's teams are known as the ___ Eagles.
I. The Erik Fisher ___ Dream
J. Paul and Joey act as ___ during the sinkhole disaster.
K. The houses tented for ___ were being robbed.
L. Paul is asked not to attend Luis's.
M. Prevents Paul from playing soccer at LWD; later "disappears"
N. Tino calls Paul this, letting him know everything is good in their friendship.
O. Paul finds a file on his dad's computer about Erik's ___ offers.
P. Paul's sport
Q. Someone smears this in Paul's face, causing him to start a fight.
R. His older brother gets all the attention of his parents.
S. Paul and his mom are shocked to see THEY play on the soccer team.
T. Tino and Victor go to the ___ ceremony to get revenge on Erik.
U. State where Paul and his family move to at the start of the novel
V. Position on the soccer team Paul has always played in the past
W. Paul prepares a statement for the ___ explaining what he witnessed.
X. Paul's mom wants practice moved to this time of day.
Y. Paul's are not interested in Erik's football achievements and plans.

Tangerine Matching 2 Answer Key

D - 1. STORAGE	A. Paul helps the Cruz family care for their tangerines during the ___.
H - 2. WAR	B. Shows Paul around school on the first day
P - 3. SOCCER	C. Antoine's little sister who plays on Paul's soccer team
J - 4. HEROES	D. Paul's mom finds the stolen goods in the ___ unit.
Q - 5. MUD	E. Coach who participated in the Olympics for track and field
X - 6. MORNING	F. Cause of Luis's death
U - 7. FLORIDA	G. Does severe damage to Lake Windsor Middle School
V - 8. GOALIE	H. Tangerine's teams are known as the ___ Eagles.
N - 9. BROTHER	I. The Erik Fisher ___ Dream
R - 10. PAUL	J. Paul and Joey act as ___ during the sinkhole disaster.
F - 11. ANEURYSM	K. The houses tented for ___ were being robbed.
A - 12. FREEZE	L. Paul is asked not to attend Luis's.
I - 13. FOOTBALL	M. Prevents Paul from playing soccer at LWD; later "disappears"
S - 14. GIRLS	N. Tino calls Paul this, letting him know everything is good in their friendship.
G - 15. SINKHOLE	O. Paul finds a file on his dad's computer about Erik's ___ offers.
T - 16. AWARD	P. Paul's sport
B - 17. THERESA	Q. Someone smears this in Paul's face, causing him to start a fight.
K - 18. TERMITES	R. His older brother gets all the attention of his parents.
C - 19. SHANDRA	S. Paul and his mom are shocked to see THEY play on the soccer team.
E - 20. BRIGHT	T. Tino and Victor go to the ___ ceremony to get revenge on Erik.
W - 21. POLICE	U. State where Paul and his family move to at the start of the novel
O - 22. SCHOLARSHIP	V. Position on the soccer team Paul has always played in the past
M - 23. IEP	W. Paul prepares a statement for the ___ explaining what he witnessed.
Y - 24. GRANDPARENTS	X. Paul's mom wants practice moved to this time of day.
L - 25. FUNERAL	Y. Paul's are not interested in Erik's football achievements and plans.

Tangerine Matching 3

___ 1. TREE
___ 2. HOUSTON
___ 3. PAUL
___ 4. MARS
___ 5. FISHER
___ 6. FOOTBALL
___ 7. FUNERAL
___ 8. SHANDRA
___ 9. SINKHOLE
___ 10. FREEZE
___ 11. ARTHUR
___ 12. MOSQUITOS
___ 13. SOCCER
___ 14. EXPELLED
___ 15. STORAGE
___ 16. FLORIDA
___ 17. AWARD
___ 18. ANEURYSM
___ 19. SCHOLARSHIP
___ 20. JOEY
___ 21. TERMITES
___ 22. ANTOINE
___ 23. MORNING
___ 24. HEROES
___ 25. PUNCH

A. Cause of Luis's death
B. The Erik Fisher ___ Dream
C. Tino and Victor go to the ___ ceremony to get revenge on Erik.
D. The houses tented for ___ were being robbed.
E. Side effect of soaking the fields in water to get rid of the fires
F. Person who pulls the ball away from Erik as he goes to kick for a last minute play
G. Paul helps the Cruz family care for their tangerines during the ___.
H. Paul thinks his dad saw Erik ___ Tino, but he did nothing.
I. Paul's mom wants practice moved to this time of day.
J. Paul's nickname at Tangerine
K. Erik's sidekick
L. Does severe damage to Lake Windsor Middle School
M. Paul finds a file on his dad's computer about Erik's ___ offers.
N. Transfers to Tangerine Middle School and hates it
O. Paul gets ___ from school for his actions at the award ceremony.
P. Paul's nickname at Lake Windsor
Q. State where Paul and his family move to at the start of the novel
R. His older brother gets all the attention of his parents.
S. Luis hurts his leg permanently from falling out of one.
T. Former home of the Fisher family
U. Antoine's little sister who plays on Paul's soccer team
V. Paul and Joey act as ___ during the sinkhole disaster.
W. Paul's mom finds the stolen goods in the ___ unit.
X. Paul's sport
Y. Paul is asked not to attend Luis's.

Tangerine Matching 3 Answer Key

S - 1. TREE
T - 2. HOUSTON
R - 3. PAUL
P - 4. MARS
J - 5. FISHER
B - 6. FOOTBALL
Y - 7. FUNERAL
U - 8. SHANDRA
L - 9. SINKHOLE
G - 10. FREEZE
K - 11. ARTHUR
E - 12. MOSQUITOS
X - 13. SOCCER
O - 14. EXPELLED
W - 15. STORAGE
Q - 16. FLORIDA
C - 17. AWARD
A - 18. ANEURYSM
M - 19. SCHOLARSHIP
N - 20. JOEY
D - 21. TERMITES
F - 22. ANTOINE
I - 23. MORNING
V - 24. HEROES
H - 25. PUNCH

A. Cause of Luis's death
B. The Erik Fisher ___ Dream
C. Tino and Victor go to the ___ ceremony to get revenge on Erik.
D. The houses tented for ___ were being robbed.
E. Side effect of soaking the fields in water to get rid of the fires
F. Person who pulls the ball away from Erik as he goes to kick for a last minute play
G. Paul helps the Cruz family care for their tangerines during the ___.
H. Paul thinks his dad saw Erik ___ Tino, but he did nothing.
I. Paul's mom wants practice moved to this time of day.
J. Paul's nickname at Tangerine
K. Erik's sidekick
L. Does severe damage to Lake Windsor Middle School
M. Paul finds a file on his dad's computer about Erik's ___ offers.
N. Transfers to Tangerine Middle School and hates it
O. Paul gets ___ from school for his actions at the award ceremony.
P. Paul's nickname at Lake Windsor
Q. State where Paul and his family move to at the start of the novel
R. His older brother gets all the attention of his parents.
S. Luis hurts his leg permanently from falling out of one.
T. Former home of the Fisher family
U. Antoine's little sister who plays on Paul's soccer team
V. Paul and Joey act as ___ during the sinkhole disaster.
W. Paul's mom finds the stolen goods in the ___ unit.
X. Paul's sport
Y. Paul is asked not to attend Luis's.

Copyrighted

Tangerine Matching 4

___ 1. ARTHUR
___ 2. SHANDRA
___ 3. TINO
___ 4. FUNERAL
___ 5. LIGHTNING
___ 6. JOEY
___ 7. PUNCH
___ 8. FLASHBACKS
___ 9. FREEZE
___ 10. MUD
___ 11. MOSQUITOS
___ 12. PAUL
___ 13. HENRY
___ 14. DAWN
___ 15. NULLIFIES
___ 16. GOALIE
___ 17. TERMITES
___ 18. ANTOINE
___ 19. BLACKJACK
___ 20. WAR
___ 21. FLORIDA
___ 22. HEROES
___ 23. POLICE
___ 24. TREE
___ 25. STORAGE

A. The houses tented for ___ were being robbed.
B. Paul and Joey act as ___ during the sinkhole disaster.
C. Paul is asked not to attend Luis's.
D. Theresa, Tino, and ___ all work with Paul on a school project.
E. Side effect of soaking the fields in water to get rid of the fires
F. Antoine's little sister who plays on Paul's soccer team
G. Luis hurts his leg permanently from falling out of one.
H. Person who pulls the ball away from Erik as he goes to kick for a last minute play
I. State where Paul and his family move to at the start of the novel
J. Tangerine's teams are known as the ___ Eagles.
K. Arthur uses it to hit Luis.
L. Paul prepares a statement for the ___ explaining what he witnessed.
M. Someone smears this in Paul's face, causing him to start a fight.
N. The county ___ all LW victories in which Antoine played.
O. Erik's sidekick
P. Transfers to Tangerine Middle School and hates it
Q. Paul thinks his dad saw Erik ___ Tino, but he did nothing.
R. Kills Mike Castello
S. Luis creates a tangerine called the Golden ___.
T. Paul's mom finds the stolen goods in the ___ unit.
U. Paul occasionally has these, about the past.
V. His older brother gets all the attention of his parents.
W. Paul helps the Cruz family care for their tangerines during the ___.
X. Starts a fight with Joey over a comment he made about Luis
Y. Position on the soccer team Paul has always played in the past

Tangerine Matching 4 Answer Key

- O - 1. ARTHUR
- F - 2. SHANDRA
- X - 3. TINO
- C - 4. FUNERAL
- R - 5. LIGHTNING
- P - 6. JOEY
- Q - 7. PUNCH
- U - 8. FLASHBACKS
- W - 9. FREEZE
- M - 10. MUD
- E - 11. MOSQUITOS
- V - 12. PAUL
- D - 13. HENRY
- S - 14. DAWN
- N - 15. NULLIFIES
- Y - 16. GOALIE
- A - 17. TERMITES
- H - 18. ANTOINE
- K - 19. BLACKJACK
- J - 20. WAR
- I - 21. FLORIDA
- B - 22. HEROES
- L - 23. POLICE
- G - 24. TREE
- T - 25. STORAGE

A. The houses tented for ___ were being robbed.
B. Paul and Joey act as ___ during the sinkhole disaster.
C. Paul is asked not to attend Luis's.
D. Theresa, Tino, and ___ all work with Paul on a school project.
E. Side effect of soaking the fields in water to get rid of the fires
F. Antoine's little sister who plays on Paul's soccer team
G. Luis hurts his leg permanently from falling out of one.
H. Person who pulls the ball away from Erik as he goes to kick for a last minute play
I. State where Paul and his family move to at the start of the novel
J. Tangerine's teams are known as the ___ Eagles.
K. Arthur uses it to hit Luis.
L. Paul prepares a statement for the ___ explaining what he witnessed.
M. Someone smears this in Paul's face, causing him to start a fight.
N. The county ___ all LW victories in which Antoine played.
O. Erik's sidekick
P. Transfers to Tangerine Middle School and hates it
Q. Paul thinks his dad saw Erik ___ Tino, but he did nothing.
R. Kills Mike Castello
S. Luis creates a tangerine called the Golden ___.
T. Paul's mom finds the stolen goods in the ___ unit.
U. Paul occasionally has these, about the past.
V. His older brother gets all the attention of his parents.
W. Paul helps the Cruz family care for their tangerines during the ___.
X. Starts a fight with Joey over a comment he made about Luis
Y. Position on the soccer team Paul has always played in the past

Tangerine Magic Squares 1

Match the definition with the vocabulary word. Put your answers in the magic squares below. When your answers are correct, all columns and rows will add to the same number.

A. FISHER
B. THERESA
C. HEROES
D. TINO
E. OSPREYS
F. SCHOLARSHIP
G. GRANDPARENTS
H. GOALIE
I. IEP
J. BUS
K. MUD
L. FOOTBALL
M. TERMITES
N. NULLIFIES
O. BLACKJACK
P. MORNING

1. Paul's nickname at Tangerine
2. The county ___ all LW victories in which Antoine played.
3. Being on the ___ at Lake Windsor means you get to play the away games.
4. Cause the coy in the pond to disappear
5. Paul's are not interested in Erik's football achievements and plans.
6. The Erik Fisher ___ Dream
7. Paul's mom wants practice moved to this time of day.
8. Paul and Joey act as ___ during the sinkhole disaster.
9. Arthur uses it to hit Luis.
10. Starts a fight with Joey over a comment he made about Luis
11. Position on the soccer team Paul has always played in the past
12. Someone smears this in Paul's face, causing him to start a fight.
13. Prevents Paul from playing soccer at LWD; later "disappears"
14. Paul finds a file on his dad's computer about Erik's ___ offers.
15. Shows Paul around school on the first day
16. The houses tented for ___ were being robbed.

A=	B=	C=	D=
E=	F=	G=	H=
I=	J=	K=	L=
M=	N=	O=	P=

Tangerine Magic Squares 1 Answer Key

Match the definition with the vocabulary word. Put your answers in the magic squares below. When your answers are correct, all columns and rows will add to the same number.

A. FISHER
B. THERESA
C. HEROES
D. TINO
E. OSPREYS
F. SCHOLARSHIP
G. GRANDPARENTS
H. GOALIE
I. IEP
J. BUS
K. MUD
L. FOOTBALL
M. TERMITES
N. NULLIFIES
O. BLACKJACK
P. MORNING

1. Paul's nickname at Tangerine
2. The county ___ all LW victories in which Antoine played.
3. Being on the ___ at Lake Windsor means you get to play the away games.
4. Cause the coy in the pond to disappear
5. Paul's are not interested in Erik's football achievements and plans.
6. The Erik Fisher ___ Dream
7. Paul's mom wants practice moved to this time of day.
8. Paul and Joey act as ___ during the sinkhole disaster.
9. Arthur uses it to hit Luis.
10. Starts a fight with Joey over a comment he made about Luis
11. Position on the soccer team Paul has always played in the past
12. Someone smears this in Paul's face, causing him to start a fight.
13. Prevents Paul from playing soccer at LWD; later "disappears"
14. Paul finds a file on his dad's computer about Erik's ___ offers.
15. Shows Paul around school on the first day
16. The houses tented for ___ were being robbed.

A=1	B=15	C=8	D=10
E=4	F=14	G=5	H=11
I=13	J=3	K=12	L=6
M=16	N=2	O=9	P=7

Copyrighted

Tangerine Magic Squares 2

Match the definition with the vocabulary word. Put your answers in the magic squares below. When your answers are correct, all columns and rows will add to the same number.

A. TERMITES
B. BROTHER
C. FOOTBALL
D. MORNING
E. ANTOINE
F. BLACKJACK
G. ANEURYSM
H. PUNCH
I. POLICE
J. HENRY
K. JOEY
L. FLORIDA
M. BRIGHT
N. NULLIFIES
O. MOSQUITOS
P. RELIEVED

1. The Erik Fisher ___ Dream
2. Theresa, Tino, and ___ all work with Paul on a school project.
3. Arthur uses it to hit Luis.
4. Side effect of soaking the fields in water to get rid of the fires
5. How Paul says he would feel if his brother died
6. Person who pulls the ball away from Erik as he goes to kick for a last minute play
7. Paul prepares a statement for the ___ explaining what he witnessed.
8. Paul's mom wants practice moved to this time of day.
9. Coach who participated in the Olympics for track and field
10. Paul thinks his dad saw Erik ___ Tino, but he did nothing.
11. State where Paul and his family move to at the start of the novel
12. The houses tented for ___ were being robbed.
13. Tino calls Paul this, letting him know everything is good in their friendship.
14. Transfers to Tangerine Middle School and hates it
15. Cause of Luis's death
16. The county ___ all LW victories in which Antoine played.

A=	B=	C=	D=
E=	F=	G=	H=
I=	J=	K=	L=
M=	N=	O=	P=

Tangerine Magic Squares 2 Answer Key

Match the definition with the vocabulary word. Put your answers in the magic squares below. When your answers are correct, all columns and rows will add to the same number.

A. TERMITES
B. BROTHER
C. FOOTBALL
D. MORNING
E. ANTOINE
F. BLACKJACK
G. ANEURYSM
H. PUNCH
I. POLICE
J. HENRY
K. JOEY
L. FLORIDA
M. BRIGHT
N. NULLIFIES
O. MOSQUITOS
P. RELIEVED

1. The Erik Fisher ___ Dream
2. Theresa, Tino, and ___ all work with Paul on a school project.
3. Arthur uses it to hit Luis.
4. Side effect of soaking the fields in water to get rid of the fires
5. How Paul says he would feel if his brother died
6. Person who pulls the ball away from Erik as he goes to kick for a last minute play
7. Paul prepares a statement for the ___ explaining what he witnessed.
8. Paul's mom wants practice moved to this time of day.
9. Coach who participated in the Olympics for track and field
10. Paul thinks his dad saw Erik ___ Tino, but he did nothing.
11. State where Paul and his family move to at the start of the novel
12. The houses tented for ___ were being robbed.
13. Tino calls Paul this, letting him know everything is good in their friendship.
14. Transfers to Tangerine Middle School and hates it
15. Cause of Luis's death
16. The county ___ all LW victories in which Antoine played.

A=12	B=13	C=1	D=8
E=6	F=3	G=15	H=10
I=7	J=2	K=14	L=11
M=9	N=16	O=4	P=5

Tangerine Magic Squares 3

Match the definition with the vocabulary word. Put your answers in the magic squares below. When your answers are correct, all columns and rows will add to the same number.

A. ECLIPSE
B. MUD
C. LIGHTNING
D. THERESA
E. BUS
F. MORNING
G. GOGGLES
H. GRANDPARENTS
I. PAUL
J. MUCK
K. GOALIE
L. SHANDRA
M. BRIGHT
N. TERMITES
O. HOUSTON
P. ANEURYSM

1. Paul's are not interested in Erik's football achievements and plans.
2. Coach who participated in the Olympics for track and field
3. Someone smears this in Paul's face, causing him to start a fight.
4. Position on the soccer team Paul has always played in the past
5. This type of fire is continuously burning behind Paul's house.
6. Kills Mike Castello
7. Cause of Luis's death
8. Being on the ___ at Lake Windsor means you get to play the away games.
9. Former home of the Fisher family
10. Paul's mom wants practice moved to this time of day.
11. His older brother gets all the attention of his parents.
12. Shows Paul around school on the first day
13. Paul tells people he looked at an ___ for too long, causing damage to his eyes.
14. Antoine's little sister who plays on Paul's soccer team
15. Paul wears these on his eyes while playing soccer
16. The houses tented for ___ were being robbed.

A=	B=	C=	D=
E=	F=	G=	H=
I=	J=	K=	L=
M=	N=	O=	P=

Tangerine Magic Squares 3 Answer Key

Match the definition with the vocabulary word. Put your answers in the magic squares below. When your answers are correct, all columns and rows will add to the same number.

A. ECLIPSE
B. MUD
C. LIGHTNING
D. THERESA
E. BUS
F. MORNING
G. GOGGLES
H. GRANDPARENTS
I. PAUL
J. MUCK
K. GOALIE
L. SHANDRA
M. BRIGHT
N. TERMITES
O. HOUSTON
P. ANEURYSM

1. Paul's are not interested in Erik's football achievements and plans.
2. Coach who participated in the Olympics for track and field
3. Someone smears this in Paul's face, causing him to start a fight.
4. Position on the soccer team Paul has always played in the past
5. This type of fire is continuously burning behind Paul's house.
6. Kills Mike Castello
7. Cause of Luis's death
8. Being on the ___ at Lake Windsor means you get to play the away games.
9. Former home of the Fisher family
10. Paul's mom wants practice moved to this time of day.
11. His older brother gets all the attention of his parents.
12. Shows Paul around school on the first day
13. Paul tells people he looked at an ___ for too long, causing damage to his eyes.
14. Antoine's little sister who plays on Paul's soccer team
15. Paul wears these on his eyes while playing soccer
16. The houses tented for ___ were being robbed.

A=13	B=3	C=6	D=12
E=8	F=10	G=15	H=1
I=11	J=5	K=4	L=14
M=2	N=16	O=9	P=7

Tangerine Magic Squares 4

Match the definition with the vocabulary word. Put your answers in the magic squares below. When your answers are correct, all columns and rows will add to the same number.

A. AWARD
B. CARNIVAL
C. POLICE
D. PUNCH
E. BROTHER
F. RELIEVED
G. THERESA
H. FUNERAL
I. ANTOINE
J. ANEURYSM
K. GIRLS
L. TERMITES
M. BLACKJACK
N. MARS
O. HOUSTON
P. FOOTBALL

1. Paul's nickname at Lake Windsor
2. Shows Paul around school on the first day
3. The houses tented for ___ were being robbed.
4. Tino and Victor go to the ___ ceremony to get revenge on Erik.
5. Paul and his mom are shocked to see THEY play on the soccer team.
6. Paul rats out the Tangerine soccer players for vandalizing an exhibit at the ___.
7. Arthur uses it to hit Luis.
8. Paul is asked not to attend Luis's.
9. Tino calls Paul this, letting him know everything is good in their friendship.
10. The Erik Fisher ___ Dream
11. Paul prepares a statement for the ___ explaining what he witnessed.
12. Cause of Luis's death
13. Paul thinks his dad saw Erik ___ Tino, but he did nothing.
14. Person who pulls the ball away from Erik as he goes to kick for a last minute play
15. How Paul says he would feel if his brother died
16. Former home of the Fisher family

A=	B=	C=	D=
E=	F=	G=	H=
I=	J=	K=	L=
M=	N=	O=	P=

Tangerine Magic Squares 4 Answer Key

Match the definition with the vocabulary word. Put your answers in the magic squares below. When your answers are correct, all columns and rows will add to the same number.

A. AWARD
B. CARNIVAL
C. POLICE
D. PUNCH
E. BROTHER
F. RELIEVED
G. THERESA
H. FUNERAL
I. ANTOINE
J. ANEURYSM
K. GIRLS
L. TERMITES
M. BLACKJACK
N. MARS
O. HOUSTON
P. FOOTBALL

1. Paul's nickname at Lake Windsor
2. Shows Paul around school on the first day
3. The houses tented for ___ were being robbed.
4. Tino and Victor go to the ___ ceremony to get revenge on Erik.
5. Paul and his mom are shocked to see THEY play on the soccer team.
6. Paul rats out the Tangerine soccer players for vandalizing an exhibit at the ___.
7. Arthur uses it to hit Luis.
8. Paul is asked not to attend Luis's.
9. Tino calls Paul this, letting him know everything is good in their friendship.
10. The Erik Fisher ___ Dream
11. Paul prepares a statement for the ___ explaining what he witnessed.
12. Cause of Luis's death
13. Paul thinks his dad saw Erik ___ Tino, but he did nothing.
14. Person who pulls the ball away from Erik as he goes to kick for a last minute play
15. How Paul says he would feel if his brother died
16. Former home of the Fisher family

A=4	B=6	C=11	D=13
E=9	F=15	G=2	H=8
I=14	J=12	K=5	L=3
M=7	N=1	O=16	P=10

Tangerine Word Search 1

```
F G B K M M O S Q U I T O S R S B
I T L E P U M O Q L R F V B E N S
S R A R U S D C G G Y B R O L X A
H Z C R N T F C Z B R W H E I S L
E T K I C K E E A C N S A K E A A
R E J T H G I R B Y E O J R V Z R
E C A F T W D J M N H Q E I E V E
L L C Z O N G N I I P H N M D L N
O I K V A O O O F E T R E O B W U
H P R H G T T F I O A E G R N U F
K S S G S N Q B R C K O S N O E S
N E L U A P O B A W A R D I M E Z
I E O V B N F S H L Q T X N A R S
S H Q M I W Z G I R L S C G R T W
R U H T R A D E A N E U R Y S M F
```

Antoine's little sister who plays on Paul's soccer team (7)
Arthur uses it to hit Luis. (9)
Being on the ___ at Lake Windsor means you get to play the away games. (3)
Cause of Luis's death (8)
Coach who participated in the Olympics for track and field (6)
Does severe damage to Lake Windsor Middle School (8)
Erik's sidekick (6)
Former home of the Fisher family (7)
Girl who likes Paul (5)
His older brother gets all the attention of his parents. (4)
How Paul says he would feel if his brother died (8)
Joey tries to take these off of his brother. (5)
Luis hurts his leg permanently from falling out of one. (4)
Paul and Joey act as ___ during the sinkhole disaster. (6)
Paul and his mom are shocked to see THEY play on the soccer team. (5)
Paul helps the Cruz family care for their tangerines during the ___. (6)
Paul is asked not to attend Luis's. (7)
Paul rats out the Tangerine soccer players for vandalizing an exhibit at the ___. (8)
Paul tells people he looked at an ___ for too long, causing damage to his eyes. (7)
Paul thinks his dad saw Erik ___ Tino, but he did nothing. (5)

Paul wears these on his eyes while playing soccer. (7)
Paul's mom wants practice moved to this time of day. (7)
Paul's nickname at Lake Windsor (4)
Paul's nickname at Tangerine (6)
Paul's sport (6)
Person who pulls the ball away from Erik as he goes to kick for a last minute play (7)
Position on the soccer team Paul has always played in the past (6)
Prevents Paul from playing soccer at LWD; later "disappears" (3)
Shows Paul around school on the first day (7)
Side effect of soaking the fields in water to get rid of the fires (9)
Someone smears this in Paul's face, causing him to start a fight. (3)
Starts a fight with Joey over a comment he made about Luis (4)
Tangerine's teams are known as the ___ Eagles. (3)
The Erik Fisher ___ Dream (8)
The houses tented for ___ were being robbed. (8)
Theresa, Tino, and ___ all work with Paul on a school project. (5)
Tino and Victor go to the ___ ceremony to get revenge on Erik. (5)
Tino calls Paul this, letting him know everything is good in their friendship. (7)
Transfers to Tangerine Middle School and hates it (4)

Tangerine Word Search 1 Answer Key

```
F     B K M M O S Q U I T O S R S
I     L E P U   O       F     E
S     A R U   D C       R O   L A
H     C R N T   C       W H E I S
E     K I C   E E     A N S A E A A
R   E J T H G I R B Y E O J R V Z R
E   C A F     D     M N H E I E E
L   L C   O N G N I P H N M D   N
O   I K   A O O   E T R E O B   U
H   P   H G T T   I O A E G R   U F
K   S S G S N   B R C   O S N O E S
N   E L U A P O B A W A R D I M E
I   E O     N       L       N A R S
S   H       I     G I R L S   G R T
R   U H T R A     E A N E U R Y S M
```

Antoine's little sister who plays on Paul's soccer team (7)

Arthur uses it to hit Luis. (9)

Being on the ___ at Lake Windsor means you get to play the away games. (3)

Cause of Luis's death (8)

Coach who participated in the Olympics for track and field (6)

Does severe damage to Lake Windsor Middle School (8)

Erik's sidekick (6)

Former home of the Fisher family (7)

Girl who likes Paul (5)

His older brother gets all the attention of his parents. (4)

How Paul says he would feel if his brother died (8)

Joey tries to take these off of his brother. (5)

Luis hurts his leg permanently from falling out of one. (4)

Paul and Joey act as ___ during the sinkhole disaster. (6)

Paul and his mom are shocked to see THEY play on the soccer team. (5)

Paul helps the Cruz family care for their tangerines during the ___. (6)

Paul is asked not to attend Luis's. (7)

Paul rats out the Tangerine soccer players for vandalizing an exhibit at the ___. (8)

Paul tells people he looked at an ___ for too long, causing damage to his eyes. (7)

Paul thinks his dad saw Erik ___ Tino, but he did nothing. (5)

Paul wears these on his eyes while playing soccer. (7)

Paul's mom wants practice moved to this time of day. (7)

Paul's nickname at Lake Windsor (4)

Paul's nickname at Tangerine (6)

Paul's sport (6)

Person who pulls the ball away from Erik as he goes to kick for a last minute play (7)

Position on the soccer team Paul has always played in the past (6)

Prevents Paul from playing soccer at LWD; later "disappears" (3)

Shows Paul around school on the first day (7)

Side effect of soaking the fields in water to get rid of the fires (9)

Someone smears this in Paul's face, causing him to start a fight. (3)

Starts a fight with Joey over a comment he made about Luis (4)

Tangerine's teams are known as the ___ Eagles. (3)

The Erik Fisher ___ Dream (8)

The houses tented for ___ were being robbed. (8)

Theresa, Tino, and ___ all work with Paul on a school project. (5)

Tino and Victor go to the ___ ceremony to get revenge on Erik. (5)

Tino calls Paul this, letting him know everything is good in their friendship .(7)

Transfers to Tangerine Middle School and hates it (4)

Tangerine Word Search 2

```
B R I G H T M O S Q U I T O S S S
L C A S R U O A Y H A W N S E C O
A S N E D S R R R A R I F P T H C
C T E C S M N M D S T D S R I O C
K N U A W E I J C E H S H E M L E
J E R R H H N M O R U B O Y R A R
A R Y N A O G U H E R O E S E R D
C A S I W U J C L H Y R S G T S E
K P M V A S Y K L T F R L I A H L
W D J A R T E D A H E S R D R I L
C N P L D O Z T B H C R I S E P E
P A U L X N E R T G E R G X H G P
B R N W A D E O O K O T P H S E X
G G C L W A R P O L I C E U I F E
J G H S Z B F V F C S G B F F Y G
```

Arthur uses it to hit Luis. (9)
Being on the ___ at Lake Windsor means you get to play the away games. (3)
Cause of Luis's death (8)
Cause the coy in the pond to disappear (7)
Coach who participated in the Olympics for track and field (6)
Erik's sidekick (6)
Former home of the Fisher family (7)
Girl who likes Paul (5)
His older brother gets all the attention of his parents. (4)
Joey tries to take these off of his brother. (5)
Luis creates a tangerine called the Golden ___. (4)
Luis hurts his leg permanently from falling out of one. (4)
Paul and Joey act as ___ during the sinkhole disaster. (6)
Paul and his mom are shocked to see THEY play on the soccer team. (5)
Paul finds a file on his dad's computer about Erik's ___ offers. (11)
Paul gets ___ from school for his actions at the award ceremony. (8)
Paul helps the Cruz family care for their tangerines during the ___. (6)
Paul prepares a statement for the ___ explaining what he witnessed. (6)
Paul rats out the Tangerine soccer players for vandalizing an exhibit at the ___. (8)
Paul thinks his dad saw Erik ___ Tino, but he did nothing. (5)

Paul's are not interested in Erik's football achievements and plans. (12)
Paul's mom wants practice moved to this time of day. (7)
Paul's nickname at Lake Windsor (4)
Paul's nickname at Tangerine (6)
Paul's sport (6)
Prevents Paul from playing soccer at LWD; later "disappears" (3)
Shows Paul around school on the first day (7)
Side effect of soaking the fields in water to get rid of the fires (9)
Someone smears this in Paul's face, causing him to start a fight. (3)
Starts a fight with Joey over a comment he made about Luis (4)
State where Paul and his family move to at the start of the novel (7)
Tangerine's teams are known as the ___ Eagles. (3)
The Erik Fisher ___ Dream (8)
The houses tented for ___ were being robbed. (8)
Theresa, Tino, and ___ all work with Paul on a school project. (5)
This type of fire is continuously burning behind Paul's house. (4)
Tino and Victor go to the ___ ceremony to get revenge on Erik. (5)
Tino calls Paul this, letting him know everything is good in their friendship. (7)
Transfers to Tangerine Middle School and hates it (4)

Tangerine Word Search 2 Answer Key

Arthur uses it to hit Luis. (9)
Being on the ___ at Lake Windsor means you get to play the away games. (3)
Cause of Luis's death (8)
Cause the coy in the pond to disappear (7)
Coach who participated in the Olympics for track and field (6)
Erik's sidekick (6)
Former home of the Fisher family (7)
Girl who likes Paul (5)
His older brother gets all the attention of his parents. (4)
Joey tries to take these off of his brother. (5)
Luis creates a tangerine called the Golden ___. (4)
Luis hurts his leg permanently from falling out of one. (4)
Paul and Joey act as ___ during the sinkhole disaster. (6)
Paul and his mom are shocked to see THEY play on the soccer team. (5)
Paul finds a file on his dad's computer about Erik's ___ offers. (11)
Paul gets ___ from school for his actions at the award ceremony. (8)
Paul helps the Cruz family care for their tangerines during the ___. (6)
Paul prepares a statement for the ___ explaining what he witnessed. (6)
Paul rats out the Tangerine soccer players for vandalizing an exhibit at the ___. (8)
Paul thinks his dad saw Erik ___ Tino, but he did nothing. (5)

Paul's are not interested in Erik's football achievements and plans. (12)
Paul's mom wants practice moved to this time of day. (7)
Paul's nickname at Lake Windsor (4)
Paul's nickname at Tangerine (6)
Paul's sport (6)
Prevents Paul from playing soccer at LWD; later "disappears" (3)
Shows Paul around school on the first day (7)
Side effect of soaking the fields in water to get rid of the fires (9)
Someone smears this in Paul's face, causing him to start a fight. (3)
Starts a fight with Joey over a comment he made about Luis (4)
State where Paul and his family move to at the start of the novel (7)
Tangerine's teams are known as the ___ Eagles. (3)
The Erik Fisher ___ Dream (8)
The houses tented for ___ were being robbed. (8)
Theresa, Tino, and ___ all work with Paul on a school project. (5)
This type of fire is continuously burning behind Paul's house. (4)
Tino and Victor go to the ___ ceremony to get revenge on Erik. (5)
Tino calls Paul this, letting him know everything is good in their friendship. (7)
Transfers to Tangerine Middle School and hates it (4)

Tangerine Word Search 3

```
F U N E R A L C S R T N J Q J M L N L T
L D Y E G A R O T S E S Y I W D A U V Z
O Y L I G H T N I N T G L P C E W R G B
R R S E T H M R E T H G I R B P K G S R
I E P D U X L N W K R N H E K D V P H B
D C B Q B C R W J A P I S C V E C C O P
A C S Q X U Q A N Q O N R H G E R F E Y
V O N I T H S D N Q L R A E O M D R S H
M S S R S H P P L F I O L X G U U B I K
V G E P E A E B U N C M O P G X S C M J
J E X L R C F R D N E M H E L N V T K C
W A R E A E L R E T C A C L E F S Y O R
S T N W N R Y I E S N H S L S O E R B N
B T A V T D T S P E A Z L E X O I N R D
S R H B O R Q H U S Z T R D J T F E O Q
D G E B I E B R U M E E I M D B I H T T
Z G R H N H Y P Y R U K G B S A L C H P
P H O K E S G S H A N D R A S L L Z E F
G R E M M I P M G O A L I E S L U W R T
L D S W Z F S I N K H O L E L Y N G G D
```

ANEURYSM
ANTOINE
ARTHUR
AWARD
BRIGHT
BROTHER
BUS
DAWN
ECLIPSE
EXPELLED
FISHER
FLORIDA
FOOTBALL
FREEZE
FUNERAL
GIRLS

GOALIE
GOGGLES
GRANDPARENTS
HENRY
HEROES
HOUSTON
IEP
JOEY
KERRI
LIGHTNING
MARS
MORNING
MOSQUITOS
MUCK
MUD
NULLIFIES

OSPREYS
PAUL
POLICE
PUNCH
RELIEVED
SCHOLARSHIP
SHANDRA
SHOES
SINKHOLE
SOCCER
STORAGE
TERMITES
THERESA
TINO
TREE
WAR

Tangerine Word Search 3 Answer Key

```
F   U N E R A L       S   R                       M       L
L         E   G A R O T S   E           I       A   U
O     L I G H T N I N G L   P       E       A   R
R   R   S E T I M R E T H G I R   B   P       R       S
I   E         U           R       N   H   E   K           H
D   C     Q   B           W   A   P   I   S   V   E       O
A   C   S         U       A   N   O   R   H   G   E   R   E
      O   N   I   T       S   D       L   R   A   E   M   D   R   S
M   S   S   R       H     P   P       I   O       O   X   G   U     I
        E   P   E   A   E         U       C       M   P   G       S   C
    E         R     C   F       R     N       E       H   E       L       T   K
W   A   R   E   A   E   L   R   E       C   A       C       S   F   S   Y   O
        N   W   N   R       Y   I   E   S   N   H       L       O   E   R   B       N
    T     A       T   O       T   S   P   E   A       L       O   I   N   R
S   R   H   O       R       H   U   S   Z   E       R   D   J   T   F   E   O
D       E   I       E       R   U   M   E   I               B   I   H   T
        R   N       H       Y       R   E       G               A   L       H
        O   E       S                   U                       L   L       E
        E   S       M           S   H   A   N   D   R   A       L   U       R
        S       I                   G   O   A   L   I   E               N
                F       S   I   N   K   H   O   L   E
```

ANEURYSM
ANTOINE
ARTHUR
AWARD
BRIGHT
BROTHER
BUS
DAWN
ECLIPSE
EXPELLED
FISHER
FLORIDA
FOOTBALL
FREEZE
FUNERAL
GIRLS

GOALIE
GOGGLES
GRANDPARENTS
HENRY
HEROES
HOUSTON
IEP
JOEY
KERRI
LIGHTNING
MARS
MORNING
MOSQUITOS
MUCK
MUD
NULLIFIES

OSPREYS
PAUL
POLICE
PUNCH
RELIEVED
SCHOLARSHIP
SHANDRA
SHOES
SINKHOLE
SOCCER
STORAGE
TERMITES
THERESA
TINO
TREE
WAR

Tangerine Word Search 4

```
T E C L I P S E N I O T N A G D J O E Y
H H P H H P I G I R L S P L R R G J X Q
G F E T I L J T M G X F A Q A A P T P N
I F H R A N T A L N F R M Q N W R I E H
R E R O E B R E L I E V E D D A W N L Q
B E G E H S M W S N E N P J P X R O L L
K R W G E S A H U R E P D U A M K Y E P
F T B A N Z E F S O L E N G R M U S D B
L W R R R E E H M O C U O E K U D M X
O W O O Y T O X O B H I L G N B J C K C
R C T T D R H T E X K L L G T V C S K R
I F H S E Z M U S C N O I L S X Y H W J
D J E H F Q B W R P I P F E N E P O M J
A G R T E R M I T E S V I S R C A U S S
S C H O L A R S H I P S E P N J U S X G
Q N X T V C A N E U R Y S M P N L T K N
R N K V Y L L A B T O O F R E C C O S G
P S H A N D R A Q K L I G H T N I N G Q
F L A S H B A C K S C A R N I V A L X Y
B L A C K J A C K M O S Q U I T O S S T
```

ANEURYSM	FUNERAL	NULLIFIES
ANTOINE	GIRLS	OSPREYS
ARTHUR	GOALIE	PAUL
AWARD	GOGGLES	POLICE
BLACKJACK	GRANDPARENTS	PUNCH
BRIGHT	HENRY	RELIEVED
BROTHER	HEROES	SCHOLARSHIP
BUS	HOUSTON	SHANDRA
CARNIVAL	IEP	SHOES
DAWN	JOEY	SINKHOLE
ECLIPSE	KERRI	SOCCER
EXPELLED	LIGHTNING	STORAGE
FISHER	MARS	TERMITES
FLASHBACKS	MORNING	THERESA
FLORIDA	MOSQUITOS	TINO
FOOTBALL	MUCK	TREE
FREEZE	MUD	WAR

Tangerine Word Search 4 Answer Key

```
T E C L I P S E N I O T N A G D J O E Y
  H H       I G I R L S   L R R     X
  G   E         M G       A   A   T P
  I F   R       A   N F R     N   I E
  R E   O E   R E L I E V E D A W N L
  B E   G E H S     S N E     P     O L
  K R W G     A H U R E P   U A M   O E
  F T B A N Z E F S O L E N G R M U S D
    R R R R E E H M O C U O E   U D
    O O Y T O   O   H I L G N B   C
    R T T   R H   E   K L L G T   S K
    I H S E     U S   N O I L S   Y H
    D E H       R     I P F E   E P O
    A R T E R M I T E S     I S R A U
    S C H O L A R S H I P   E P     U S
              A N E U R Y S M       L T
              L L A B T O O F R E C C O S
    S H A N D R A     L I G H T N I N G
  F L A S H B A C K S C A R N I V A L
  B L A C K J A C K M O S Q U I T O S
```

ANEURYSM	FUNERAL	NULLIFIES
ANTOINE	GIRLS	OSPREYS
ARTHUR	GOALIE	PAUL
AWARD	GOGGLES	POLICE
BLACKJACK	GRANDPARENTS	PUNCH
BRIGHT	HENRY	RELIEVED
BROTHER	HEROES	SCHOLARSHIP
BUS	HOUSTON	SHANDRA
CARNIVAL	IEP	SHOES
DAWN	JOEY	SINKHOLE
ECLIPSE	KERRI	SOCCER
EXPELLED	LIGHTNING	STORAGE
FISHER	MARS	TERMITES
FLASHBACKS	MORNING	THERESA
FLORIDA	MOSQUITOS	TINO
FOOTBALL	MUCK	TREE
FREEZE	MUD	WAR

Tangerine Crossword 1

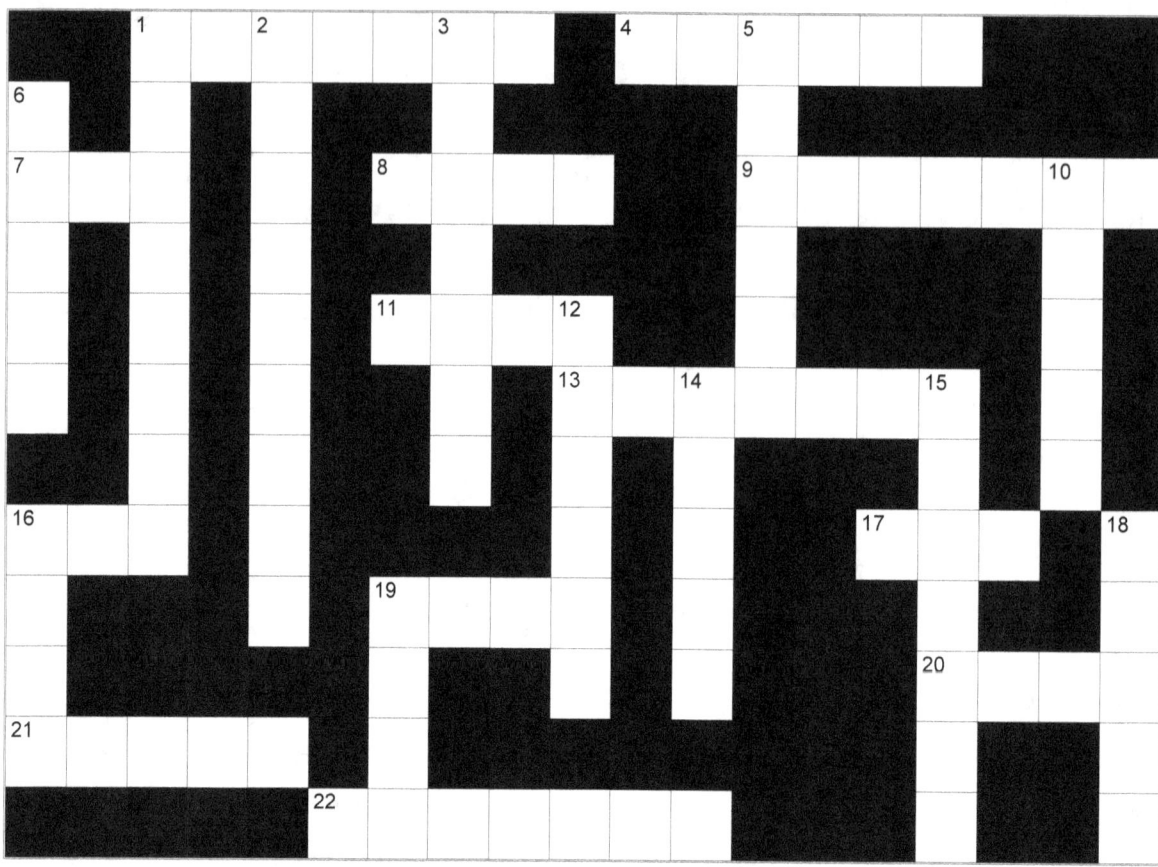

Across
1. Paul tells people he looked at an ___ for too long, causing damage to his eyes.
4. Position on the soccer team Paul has always played in the past
7. Prevents Paul from playing soccer at LWD; later "disappears"
8. Transfers to Tangerine Middle School and hates it
9. Shows Paul around school on the first day
11. Paul's nickname at Lake Windsor
13. Cause the coy in the pond to disappear
16. Someone smears this in Paul's face, causing him to start a fight.
17. Tangerine's teams are known as the ___ Eagles.
19. Luis hurts his leg permanently from falling out of one.
20. Luis creates a tangerine called the Golden ___.
21. Girl who likes Paul
22. Paul wears these on his eyes while playing soccer.

Down
1. Paul gets ___ from school for his actions at the award ceremony.
2. Kills Mike Castello
3. Paul's mom finds the stolen goods in the ___ unit.
5. Erik's sidekick
6. Paul and his mom are shocked to see THEY play on the soccer team.
10. Joey tries to take these off of his brother.
12. Paul's sport
14. Paul thinks his dad saw Erik ___ Tino, but he did nothing.
15. Antoine's little sister who plays on Paul's soccer team
16. This type of fire is continuously burning behind Paul's house.
18. Theresa, Tino, and ___ all work with Paul on a school project.
19. Starts a fight with Joey over a comment he made about Luis

Tangerine Crossword 1 Answer Key

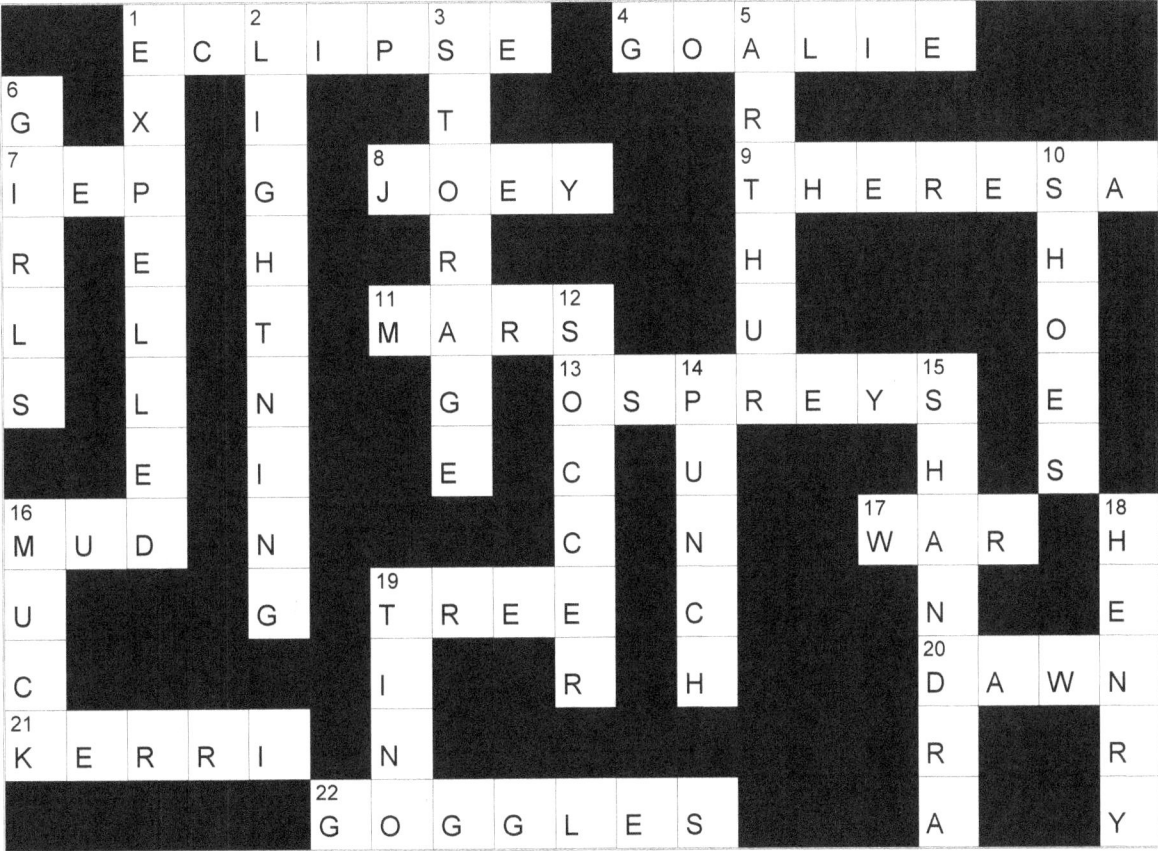

Across
1. Paul tells people he looked at an ___ for too long, causing damage to his eyes.
4. Position on the soccer team Paul has always played in the past
7. Prevents Paul from playing soccer at LWD; later "disappears"
8. Transfers to Tangerine Middle School and hates it
9. Shows Paul around school on the first day
11. Paul's nickname at Lake Windsor
13. Cause the coy in the pond to disappear
16. Someone smears this in Paul's face, causing him to start a fight.
17. Tangerine's teams are known as the ___ Eagles.
19. Luis hurts his leg permanently from falling out of one.
20. Luis creates a tangerine called the Golden ___.
21. Girl who likes Paul
22. Paul wears these on his eyes while playing soccer.

Down
1. Paul gets ___ from school for his actions at the award ceremony.
2. Kills Mike Castello
3. Paul's mom finds the stolen goods in the ___ unit.
5. Erik's sidekick
6. Paul and his mom are shocked to see THEY play on the soccer team.
10. Joey tries to take these off of his brother.
12. Paul's sport
14. Paul thinks his dad saw Erik ___ Tino, but he did nothing.
15. Antoine's little sister who plays on Paul's soccer team
16. This type of fire is continuously burning behind Paul's house.
18. Theresa, Tino, and ___ all work with Paul on a school project.
19. Starts a fight with Joey over a comment he made about Luis

Tangerine Crossword 2

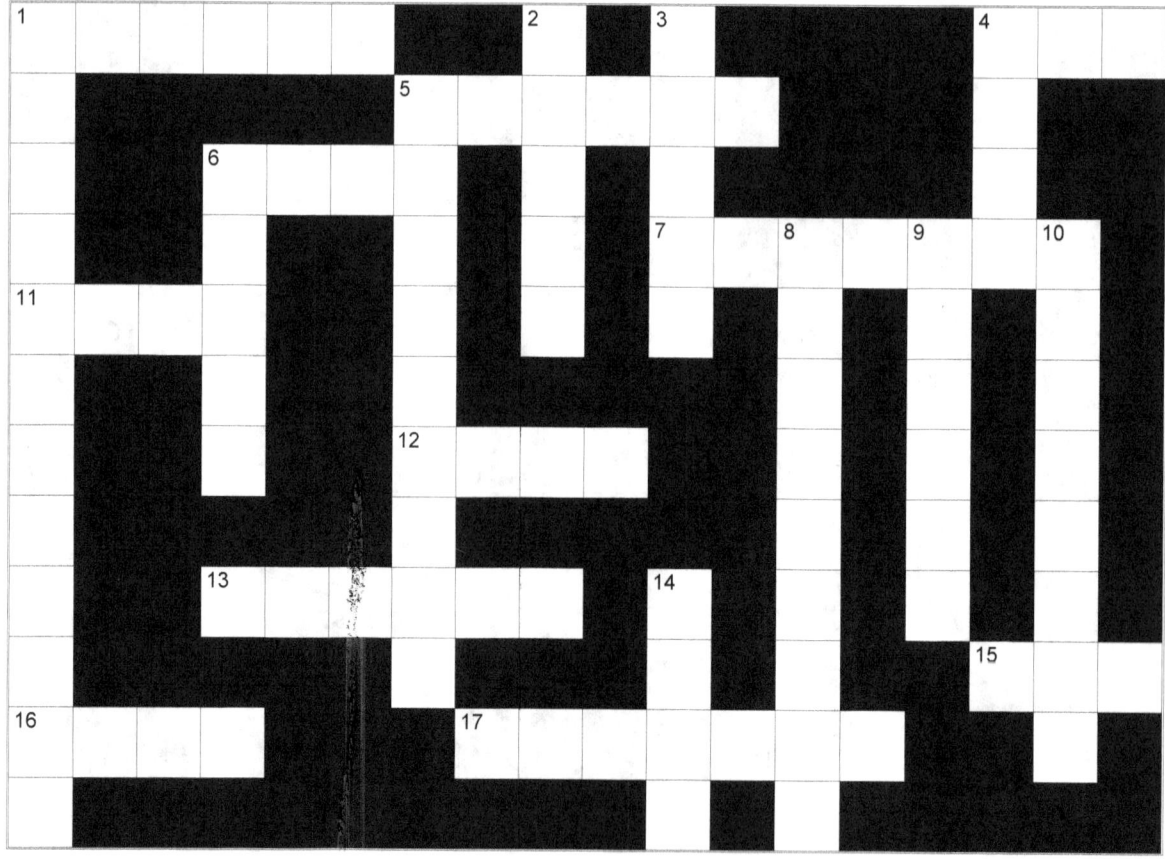

Across
1. Position on the soccer team Paul has always played in the past
4. Someone smears this in Paul's face, causing him to start a fight.
5. Coach who participated in the Olympics for track and field
6. His older brother gets all the attention of his parents.
7. Paul tells people he looked at an ___ for too long, causing damage to his eyes.
11. Luis creates a tangerine called the Golden ___.
12. Transfers to Tangerine Middle School and hates it
13. Paul's sport
15. Prevents Paul from playing soccer at LWD; later "disappears"
16. Luis hurts his leg permanently from falling out of one.
17. Paul's mom wants practice moved to this time of day.

Down
1. Paul's are not interested in Erik's football achievements and plans.
2. Paul and his mom are shocked to see THEY play on the soccer team.
3. Joey tries to take these off of his brother.
4. Paul's nickname at Lake Windsor
5. Arthur uses it to hit Luis.
6. Paul thinks his dad saw Erik ___ Tino, but he did nothing.
8. Kills Mike Castello
9. Paul prepares a statement for the ___ explaining what he witnessed.
10. Paul gets ___ from school for his actions at the award ceremony.
14. Starts a fight with Joey over a comment he made about Luis

Tangerine Crossword 2 Answer Key

Across
1. Position on the soccer team Paul has always played in the past
4. Someone smears this in Paul's face, causing him to start a fight.
5. Coach who participated in the Olympics for track and field
6. His older brother gets all the attention of his parents.
7. Paul tells people he looked at an ___ for too long, causing damage to his eyes.
11. Luis creates a tangerine called the Golden ___.
12. Transfers to Tangerine Middle School and hates it
13. Paul's sport
15. Prevents Paul from playing soccer at LWD; later "disappears"
16. Luis hurts his leg permanently from falling out of one.
17. Paul's mom wants practice moved to this time of day.

Down
1. Paul's are not interested in Erik's football achievements and plans.
2. Paul and his mom are shocked to see THEY play on the soccer team.
3. Joey tries to take these off of his brother.
4. Paul's nickname at Lake Windsor
5. Arthur uses it to hit Luis.
6. Paul thinks his dad saw Erik ___ Tino, but he did nothing.
8. Kills Mike Castello
9. Paul prepares a statement for the ___ explaining what he witnessed.
10. Paul gets ___ from school for his actions at the award ceremony.
14. Starts a fight with Joey over a comment he made about Luis

Tangerine Crossword 3

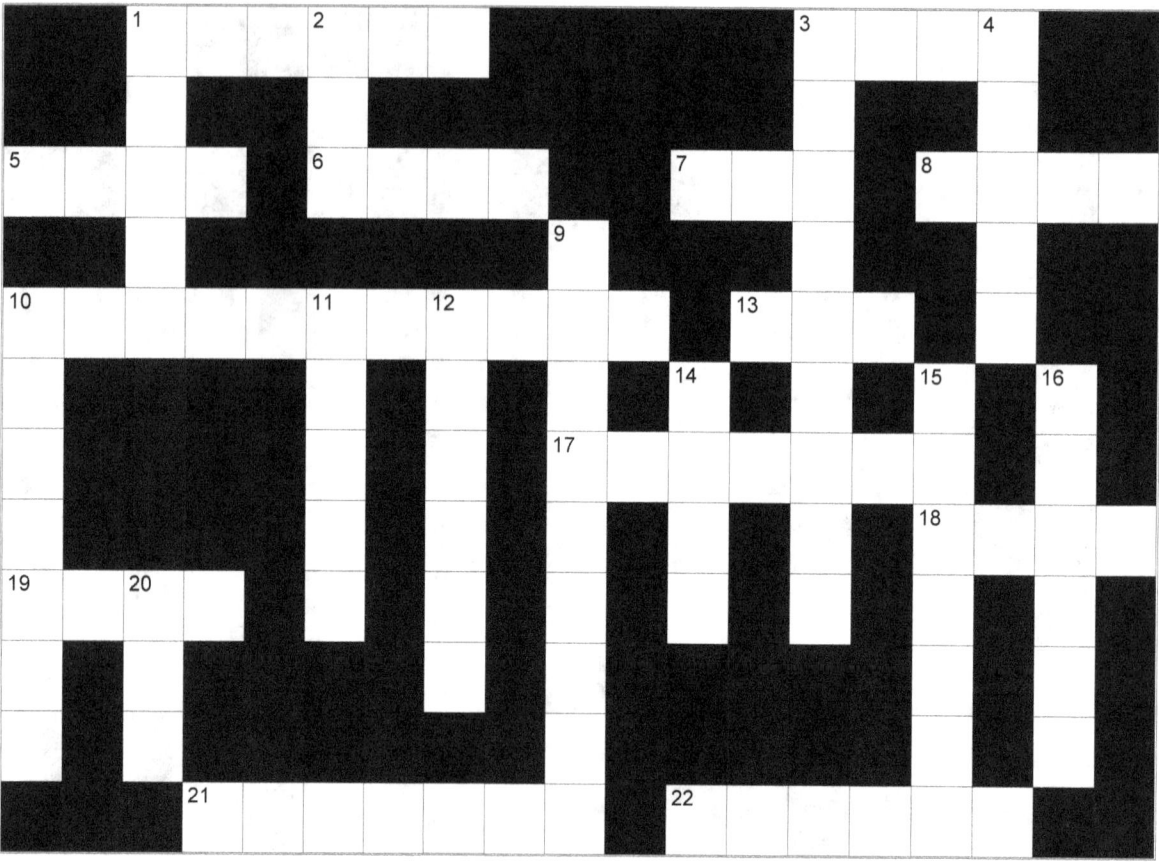

Across
1. Paul prepares a statement for the ___ explaining what he witnessed.
3. Paul's nickname at Lake Windsor
5. Starts a fight with Joey over a comment he made about Luis
6. His older brother gets all the attention of his parents.
7. Being on the ___ at Lake Windsor means you get to play the away games.
8. Transfers to Tangerine Middle School and hates it
10. Paul finds a file on his dad's computer about Erik's ___ offers.
13. Someone smears this in Paul's face, causing him to start a fight.
17. Former home of the Fisher family
18. Luis hurts his leg permanently from falling out of one.
19. Luis creates a tangerine called the Golden ___.
21. Paul's mom wants practice moved to this time of day.
22. Paul and Joey act as ___ during the sinkhole disaster.

Down
1. Paul thinks his dad saw Erik ___ Tino, but he did nothing.
2. Prevents Paul from playing soccer at LWD; later "disappears"
3. Side effect of soaking the fields in water to get rid of the fires
4. Joey tries to take these off of his brother.
9. Kills Mike Castello
10. Antoine's little sister who plays on Paul's soccer team
11. Tino and Victor go to the ___ ceremony to get revenge on Erik.
12. Paul's sport
14. This type of fire is continuously burning behind Paul's house.
15. Person who pulls the ball away from Erik as he goes to kick for a last minute play
16. Paul helps the Cruz family care for their tangerines during the ___.
20. Tangerine's teams are known as the ___ Eagles.

Tangerine Crossword 3 Answer Key

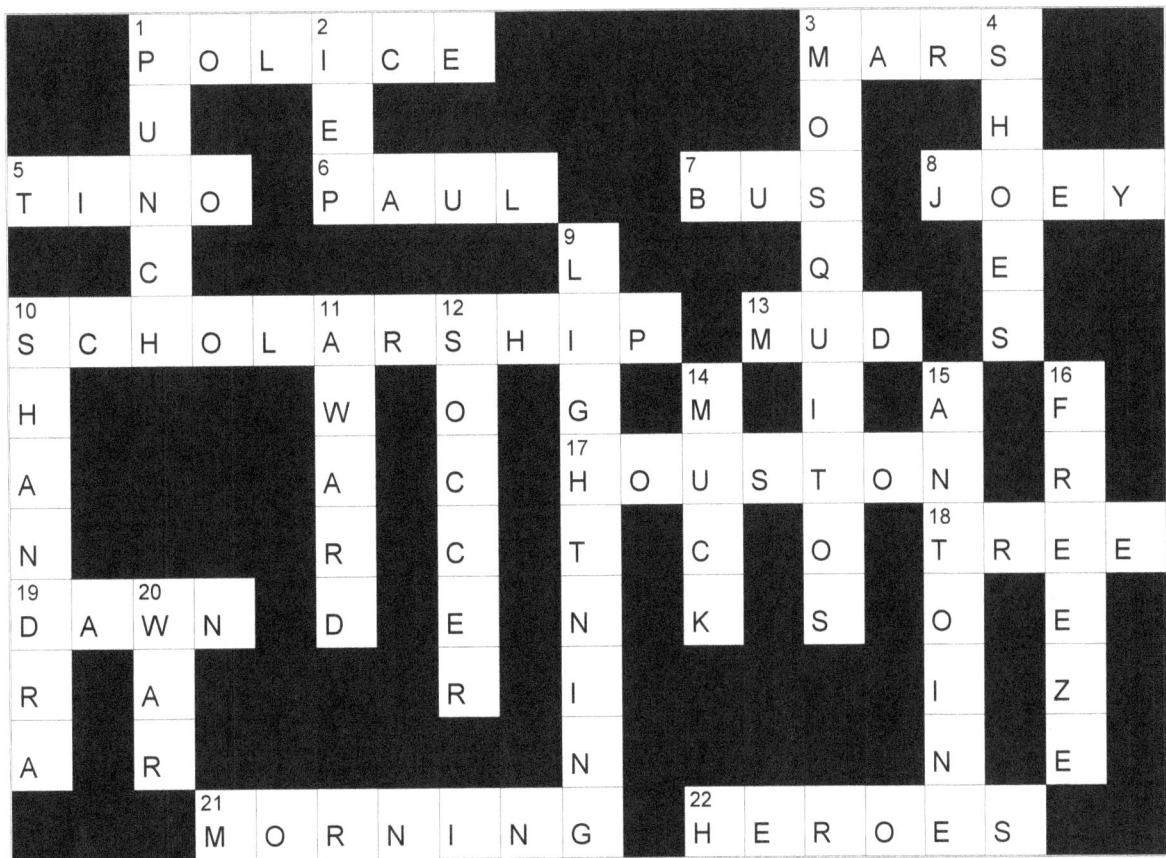

Across
1. Paul prepares a statement for the ___ explaining what he witnessed.
3. Paul's nickname at Lake Windsor
5. Starts a fight with Joey over a comment he made about Luis
6. His older brother gets all the attention of his parents.
7. Being on the ___ at Lake Windsor means you get to play the away games.
8. Transfers to Tangerine Middle School and hates it
10. Paul finds a file on his dad's computer about Erik's ___ offers.
13. Someone smears this in Paul's face, causing him to start a fight.
17. Former home of the Fisher family
18. Luis hurts his leg permanently from falling out of one.
19. Luis creates a tangerine called the Golden ___.
21. Paul's mom wants practice moved to this time of day.
22. Paul and Joey act as ___ during the sinkhole disaster.

Down
1. Paul thinks his dad saw Erik ___ Tino, but he did nothing.
2. Prevents Paul from playing soccer at LWD; later "disappears"
3. Side effect of soaking the fields in water to get rid of the fires
4. Joey tries to take these off of his brother.
9. Kills Mike Castello
10. Antoine's little sister who plays on Paul's soccer team
11. Tino and Victor go to the ___ ceremony to get revenge on Erik.
12. Paul's sport
14. This type of fire is continuously burning behind Paul's house.
15. Person who pulls the ball away from Erik as he goes to kick for a last minute play
16. Paul helps the Cruz family care for their tangerines during the ___.
20. Tangerine's teams are known as the ___ Eagles.

Tangerine Crossword 4

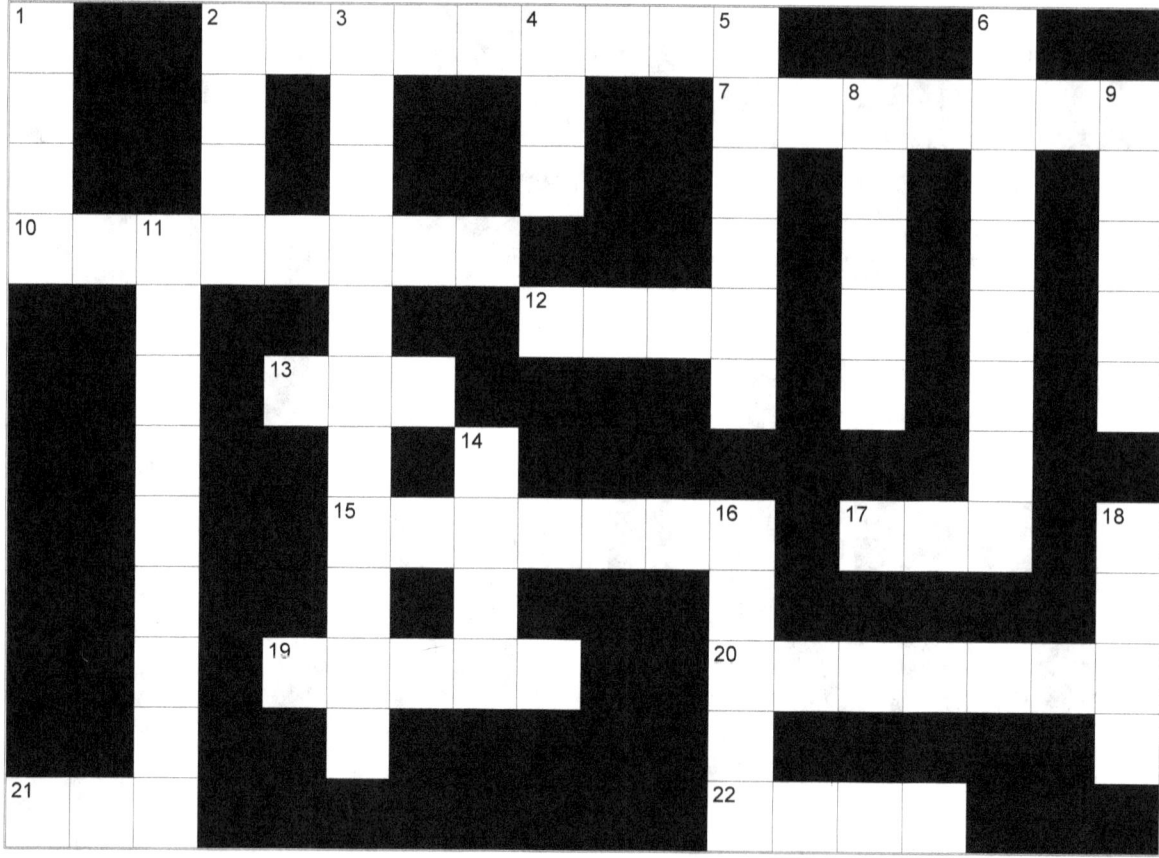

Across
2. Side effect of soaking the fields in water to get rid of the fires
7. Cause the coy in the pond to disappear
10. Does severe damage to Lake Windsor Middle School
12. Luis hurts his leg permanently from falling out of one.
13. Tangerine's teams are known as the ___ Eagles.
15. Antoine's little sister who plays on Paul's soccer team
17. Someone smears this in Paul's face, causing him to start a fight.
19. Paul and his mom are shocked to see THEY play on the soccer team.
20. Person who pulls the ball away from Erik as he goes to kick for a last minute play
21. Being on the ___ at Lake Windsor means you get to play the away games.
22. Luis creates a tangerine called the Golden ___.

Down
1. Paul's nickname at Lake Windsor
2. This type of fire is continuously burning behind Paul's house.
3. Paul finds a file on his dad's computer about Erik's ___ offers.
4. Prevents Paul from playing soccer at LWD; later "disappears"
5. Paul's sport
6. How Paul says he would feel if his brother died
8. Paul thinks his dad saw Erik ___ Tino, but he did nothing.
9. Joey tries to take these off of his brother.
11. The county ___ all LW victories in which Antoine played.
14. His older brother gets all the attention of his parents.
16. Tino and Victor go to the ___ ceremony to get revenge on Erik.
18. Transfers to Tangerine Middle School and hates it

Tangerine Crossword 4 Answer Key

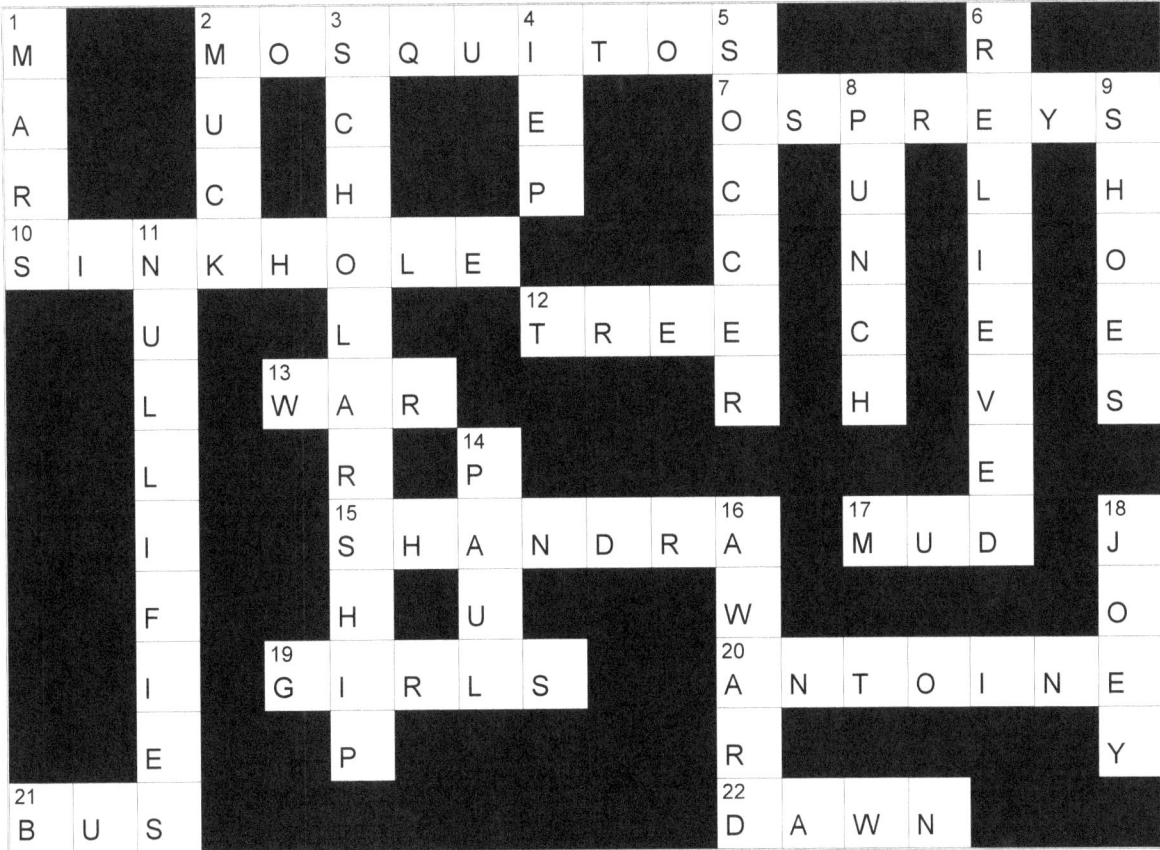

Across
2. Side effect of soaking the fields in water to get rid of the fires
7. Cause the coy in the pond to disappear
10. Does severe damage to Lake Windsor Middle School
12. Luis hurts his leg permanently from falling out of one.
13. Tangerine's teams are known as the ___ Eagles.
15. Antoine's little sister who plays on Paul's soccer team
17. Someone smears this in Paul's face, causing him to start a fight.
19. Paul and his mom are shocked to see THEY play on the soccer team.
20. Person who pulls the ball away from Erik as he goes to kick for a last minute play
21. Being on the ___ at Lake Windsor means you get to play the away games.
22. Luis creates a tangerine called the Golden ___.

Down
1. Paul's nickname at Lake Windsor
2. This type of fire is continuously burning behind Paul's house.
3. Paul finds a file on his dad's computer about Erik's ___ offers.
4. Prevents Paul from playing soccer at LWD; later "disappears"
5. Paul's sport
6. How Paul says he would feel if his brother died
8. Paul thinks his dad saw Erik ___ Tino, but he did nothing.
9. Joey tries to take these off of his brother.
11. The county ___ all LW victories in which Antoine played.
14. His older brother gets all the attention of his parents.
16. Tino and Victor go to the ___ ceremony to get revenge on Erik.
18. Transfers to Tangerine Middle School and hates it

Tangerine

MOSQUITOS	KERRI	SHANDRA	GOALIE	CARNIVAL
ARTHUR	GOGGLES	OSPREYS	BRIGHT	AWARD
BROTHER	THERESA	FREE SPACE	JOEY	RELIEVED
WAR	PUNCH	PAUL	ECLIPSE	LIGHTNING
HOUSTON	FUNERAL	SOCCER	BUS	GRANDPARENTS

Tangerine

ANTOINE	MARS	TREE	MORNING	FREEZE
ANEURYSM	HEROES	SHOES	FLORIDA	FOOTBALL
SINKHOLE	EXPELLED	FREE SPACE	TERMITES	GIRLS
MUCK	MUD	STORAGE	TINO	FLASHBACKS
NULLIFIES	FISHER	HENRY	BLACKJACK	DAWN

Tangerine

FREEZE	BLACKJACK	OSPREYS	TREE	MOSQUITOS
PUNCH	DAWN	ARTHUR	MARS	HENRY
WAR	MUD	FREE SPACE	SHANDRA	JOEY
GOALIE	TINO	NULLIFIES	KERRI	MORNING
IEP	ECLIPSE	FLASHBACKS	SCHOLARSHIP	ANEURYSM

Tangerine

SOCCER	RELIEVED	LIGHTNING	HEROES	GIRLS
GRANDPARENTS	CARNIVAL	ANTOINE	FOOTBALL	PAUL
MUCK	GOGGLES	FREE SPACE	FLORIDA	POLICE
BROTHER	TERMITES	THERESA	SHOES	AWARD
FUNERAL	HOUSTON	FISHER	SINKHOLE	STORAGE

Tangerine

MOSQUITOS	THERESA	PUNCH	DAWN	CARNIVAL
HOUSTON	STORAGE	GRANDPARENTS	GOGGLES	WAR
MUCK	FREEZE	FREE SPACE	BRIGHT	MARS
MORNING	HEROES	MUD	GOALIE	SHANDRA
FLORIDA	SHOES	RELIEVED	TINO	FLASHBACKS

Tangerine

GIRLS	SINKHOLE	FOOTBALL	TREE	FISHER
HENRY	TERMITES	BROTHER	KERRI	EXPELLED
OSPREYS	POLICE	FREE SPACE	ANTOINE	ANEURYSM
IEP	SOCCER	SCHOLARSHIP	NULLIFIES	BUS
PAUL	BLACKJACK	AWARD	ECLIPSE	LIGHTNING

Tangerine

CARNIVAL	KERRI	FLASHBACKS	FLORIDA	SINKHOLE
SHOES	DAWN	EXPELLED	HEROES	MUD
MARS	GOGGLES	FREE SPACE	BRIGHT	IEP
FISHER	GOALIE	STORAGE	MORNING	ARTHUR
FUNERAL	JOEY	HOUSTON	POLICE	BLACKJACK

Tangerine

BROTHER	LIGHTNING	SOCCER	ANTOINE	THERESA
NULLIFIES	ANEURYSM	AWARD	PUNCH	WAR
ECLIPSE	MUCK	FREE SPACE	RELIEVED	FOOTBALL
SCHOLARSHIP	BUS	GRANDPARENTS	TREE	PAUL
SHANDRA	GIRLS	FREEZE	MOSQUITOS	TERMITES

Tangerine

MOSQUITOS	HOUSTON	SINKHOLE	LIGHTNING	BLACKJACK
THERESA	TREE	ANTOINE	IEP	SOCCER
FREEZE	GOALIE	FREE SPACE	ANEURYSM	SHANDRA
FLASHBACKS	HEROES	MUCK	HENRY	FOOTBALL
POLICE	MORNING	RELIEVED	BROTHER	MUD

Tangerine

BRIGHT	DAWN	STORAGE	BUS	TINO
NULLIFIES	GIRLS	MARS	JOEY	WAR
PAUL	FLORIDA	FREE SPACE	SHOES	CARNIVAL
GRANDPARENTS	ARTHUR	TERMITES	FUNERAL	EXPELLED
GOGGLES	FISHER	AWARD	OSPREYS	PUNCH

Tangerine

TERMITES	RELIEVED	BLACKJACK	FISHER	DAWN
SINKHOLE	NULLIFIES	TINO	ARTHUR	MOSQUITOS
TREE	BUS	FREE SPACE	HENRY	LIGHTNING
GOGGLES	HOUSTON	ANEURYSM	ANTOINE	GOALIE
WAR	BRIGHT	EXPELLED	FREEZE	FLASHBACKS

Tangerine

MUD	MUCK	IEP	JOEY	PUNCH
SCHOLARSHIP	PAUL	SHOES	SHANDRA	POLICE
KERRI	HEROES	FREE SPACE	AWARD	FOOTBALL
MARS	OSPREYS	GIRLS	FUNERAL	STORAGE
MORNING	SOCCER	BROTHER	CARNIVAL	GRANDPARENTS

Tangerine

SINKHOLE	SHOES	SCHOLARSHIP	STORAGE	PUNCH
AWARD	OSPREYS	NULLIFIES	GOGGLES	ANEURYSM
BRIGHT	DAWN	FREE SPACE	TREE	BUS
ECLIPSE	CARNIVAL	ARTHUR	HEROES	THERESA
MUD	KERRI	FOOTBALL	MOSQUITOS	TERMITES

Tangerine

LIGHTNING	SOCCER	HENRY	POLICE	GOALIE
BROTHER	FLASHBACKS	ANTOINE	TINO	JOEY
FUNERAL	MARS	FREE SPACE	SHANDRA	WAR
HOUSTON	RELIEVED	FISHER	PAUL	GRANDPARENTS
IEP	MORNING	MUCK	EXPELLED	GIRLS

Tangerine

SCHOLARSHIP	MUD	FLASHBACKS	NULLIFIES	ANTOINE
HENRY	GRANDPARENTS	SINKHOLE	MOSQUITOS	TINO
BLACKJACK	ANEURYSM	FREE SPACE	STORAGE	THERESA
RELIEVED	SHOES	HEROES	DAWN	BROTHER
FUNERAL	TERMITES	CARNIVAL	EXPELLED	BRIGHT

Tangerine

JOEY	SHANDRA	FLORIDA	FREEZE	ECLIPSE
TREE	POLICE	FISHER	GOALIE	PAUL
GIRLS	MUCK	FREE SPACE	MORNING	HOUSTON
FOOTBALL	GOGGLES	PUNCH	BUS	OSPREYS
AWARD	MARS	WAR	SOCCER	IEP

Tangerine

MUCK	GIRLS	SHANDRA	TERMITES	ARTHUR
FUNERAL	POLICE	PUNCH	IEP	THERESA
GOALIE	ECLIPSE	FREE SPACE	BROTHER	AWARD
LIGHTNING	NULLIFIES	SHOES	FLORIDA	HEROES
FISHER	FREEZE	ANEURYSM	SOCCER	FLASHBACKS

Tangerine

WAR	MOSQUITOS	BUS	HOUSTON	CARNIVAL
SINKHOLE	HENRY	OSPREYS	JOEY	BLACKJACK
RELIEVED	TINO	FREE SPACE	EXPELLED	FOOTBALL
BRIGHT	PAUL	KERRI	GRANDPARENTS	DAWN
ANTOINE	STORAGE	MARS	GOGGLES	TREE

Tangerine

STORAGE	ANTOINE	ARTHUR	IEP	MUCK
NULLIFIES	BLACKJACK	DAWN	GIRLS	FLORIDA
MORNING	TINO	FREE SPACE	ECLIPSE	TERMITES
KERRI	JOEY	SHOES	WAR	AWARD
PAUL	CARNIVAL	FREEZE	FUNERAL	TREE

Tangerine

BUS	BRIGHT	POLICE	SINKHOLE	SOCCER
MOSQUITOS	HEROES	FISHER	GOGGLES	LIGHTNING
EXPELLED	ANEURYSM	FREE SPACE	MARS	BROTHER
PUNCH	OSPREYS	FLASHBACKS	MUD	THERESA
SCHOLARSHIP	GRANDPARENTS	RELIEVED	HOUSTON	FOOTBALL

Tangerine

NULLIFIES	GOGGLES	SOCCER	IEP	POLICE
TINO	PUNCH	CARNIVAL	JOEY	EXPELLED
LIGHTNING	SCHOLARSHIP	FREE SPACE	TREE	HENRY
FREEZE	MOSQUITOS	WAR	BLACKJACK	ECLIPSE
HEROES	BRIGHT	OSPREYS	FUNERAL	ARTHUR

Tangerine

DAWN	RELIEVED	FLORIDA	GRANDPARENTS	STORAGE
ANEURYSM	AWARD	SHOES	SINKHOLE	BROTHER
MORNING	KERRI	FREE SPACE	PAUL	TERMITES
SHANDRA	MUD	MARS	MUCK	FOOTBALL
BUS	GOALIE	GIRLS	FISHER	HOUSTON

Tangerine

FLORIDA	RELIEVED	OSPREYS	POLICE	SOCCER
FLASHBACKS	JOEY	ANEURYSM	SHANDRA	GOALIE
GRANDPARENTS	IEP	FREE SPACE	THERESA	BLACKJACK
MOSQUITOS	CARNIVAL	SINKHOLE	LIGHTNING	TERMITES
ECLIPSE	HENRY	MARS	BROTHER	TREE

Tangerine

NULLIFIES	FOOTBALL	ANTOINE	EXPELLED	FISHER
MUD	PAUL	MUCK	WAR	GIRLS
HOUSTON	MORNING	FREE SPACE	HEROES	STORAGE
SHOES	BUS	FUNERAL	AWARD	PUNCH
DAWN	GOGGLES	FREEZE	TINO	BRIGHT

Tangerine

PUNCH	AWARD	ANEURYSM	NULLIFIES	HOUSTON
FOOTBALL	LIGHTNING	SOCCER	ECLIPSE	GOALIE
GIRLS	OSPREYS	FREE SPACE	FLORIDA	HENRY
STORAGE	GRANDPARENTS	TREE	HEROES	SINKHOLE
RELIEVED	EXPELLED	WAR	FREEZE	FISHER

Tangerine

FUNERAL	TERMITES	MOSQUITOS	SHANDRA	CARNIVAL
SHOES	BLACKJACK	IEP	POLICE	MARS
TINO	GOGGLES	FREE SPACE	MUCK	MUD
DAWN	SCHOLARSHIP	ANTOINE	JOEY	PAUL
KERRI	FLASHBACKS	ARTHUR	BROTHER	THERESA

Tangerine

EXPELLED	FLORIDA	KERRI	DAWN	LIGHTNING
HENRY	MUD	OSPREYS	GOGGLES	BUS
HOUSTON	BROTHER	FREE SPACE	WAR	BLACKJACK
RELIEVED	FISHER	FLASHBACKS	ANEURYSM	POLICE
SINKHOLE	HEROES	GRANDPARENTS	FUNERAL	TINO

Tangerine

SOCCER	SHOES	SCHOLARSHIP	MORNING	FOOTBALL
ARTHUR	FREEZE	CARNIVAL	THERESA	STORAGE
GOALIE	NULLIFIES	FREE SPACE	ANTOINE	MOSQUITOS
JOEY	BRIGHT	SHANDRA	TERMITES	GIRLS
PAUL	IEP	PUNCH	TREE	MUCK

Tangerine

SOCCER	TREE	GRANDPARENTS	FREEZE	MARS
FISHER	STORAGE	SHOES	ARTHUR	GOGGLES
BLACKJACK	FUNERAL	FREE SPACE	NULLIFIES	OSPREYS
EXPELLED	MOSQUITOS	HOUSTON	JOEY	CARNIVAL
HEROES	RELIEVED	MORNING	KERRI	MUD

Tangerine

BUS	IEP	FOOTBALL	FLORIDA	GOALIE
TINO	SCHOLARSHIP	ANTOINE	TERMITES	THERESA
MUCK	PUNCH	FREE SPACE	ANEURYSM	PAUL
GIRLS	WAR	DAWN	SHANDRA	ECLIPSE
FLASHBACKS	POLICE	LIGHTNING	BRIGHT	AWARD

Tangerine

GRANDPARENTS	JOEY	HEROES	IEP	GIRLS
CARNIVAL	SHOES	FOOTBALL	MORNING	ECLIPSE
WAR	FUNERAL	FREE SPACE	MUCK	LIGHTNING
TERMITES	TREE	MUD	BRIGHT	STORAGE
EXPELLED	GOGGLES	ARTHUR	FLORIDA	POLICE

Tangerine

HOUSTON	BLACKJACK	BUS	BROTHER	SHANDRA
ANEURYSM	DAWN	ANTOINE	AWARD	PUNCH
OSPREYS	PAUL	FREE SPACE	KERRI	MARS
HENRY	THERESA	FLASHBACKS	TINO	SINKHOLE
MOSQUITOS	FISHER	SCHOLARSHIP	RELIEVED	FREEZE

Tangerine Vocabulary Word List

No. Word	Clue/Definition
1. ABRUPTLY	Suddenly or unexpectedly
2. ADJOURN	Suspend (as a meeting) to or until another place or time
3. AFFIDAVITS	Written statements made under oath
4. AGITATED	Upset or disturbed
5. AGONIZING	Filled with distress, suffering, or torture; worrying in a distressed way
6. ANEURYSM	A swell, almost like a bubble, in an artery; if it bursts, it is usually fatal
7. ARCHENEMY	Main enemy
8. ASTRIDE	One leg on either side of; straddling
9. BANTER	Light, teasing, playful remarks
10. BILLOWING	Moving (usually upward or outward) in a rolling, swelling motion
11. BROODED	Was in deep thought; focused attention on one subject persistently
12. CALISTHENICS	Exercises to develop muscles
13. CAPSIZING	Turning or flipping over
14. COMPREHEND	Understand
15. CONSCIENCE	One's own moral or ethical awareness of right and wrong
16. CONSTITUTES	Makes the elements or parts of
17. CONTORT	Twist into a strange shape or expression
18. CONVICTION	Fixed or firm belief
19. CONVOY	Escort; a group (as of vehicles) traveling together for convenience
20. COOPERATED	Worked together willingly and agreeably
21. CORRUGATED	Having folds, ridges, and grooves
22. CUE	Signal used to prompt an action
23. DECOY	Something or someone used to lure or mislead another into a trap
24. DESPISED	Disliked intensely; scorned; loathed
25. DILAPIDATED	Ruined or decayed from age, wear, or neglect
26. DISBELIEF	Amazement or astonishment
27. DISCLOSURE	Making facts and details evident and clear
28. DISINFECTANT	Chemical agent used to destroy bacteria
29. DISINTEGRATING	Breaking up; deteriorating; falling apart
30. DWELL	Focus one's attention on (usually a thought) for an extended period of time
31. ECLIPSE	The disappearance of the whole or a part of the sun when the moon comes between it and earth
32. ELATED	Very happy or proud; in high spirits
33. EXPLOITS	Outstanding events in which a person puts his or her strong points to the best advantage
34. FORFEIT	Surrender or give up as punishment for a crime, error, or offense
35. FUMIGATED	Subjected to smoke or fumes, usually to exterminate bugs
36. GHOULISH	Strangely cruel or monstrous
37. GNAT	Very small, biting fly
38. HASTILY	Quickly
39. HEAVE	Rise up or swell; bulge; lift
40. HORTICULTURE	The science or art of cultivating plants
41. IMPATIENT	Wanting to hurry up; not wanting to wait for something to be

	done or to happen
42. INCONSISTENT	Not regular or predictable
43. INFRACTION	Violation; breach
44. INSOLENTLY	In a way that is boldly rude or disrespectful
45. INTENTLY	With great concentration or eager attention
46. INTERVENED	Came between to mediate or help
47. IRREGULARITIES	Things that are not within the usual rules or customs
48. JEERING	Mocking, taunting, or verbally abusing
49. JITTERY	Extremely tense or nervous
50. LIABLE	Legally obligated or responsible
51. MENACING	Threatening or dangerous
52. NULLIFY	Declare something void; invalidate
53. OBLIGED	Required; bonded
54. OMINOUSLY	In a threatening way
55. OVATION	Enthusiastic, prolonged applause
56. PARALLEL	Extending in the same direction, equally distant at every point
57. PELTING	Bombarding; striking rapidly and repeatedly
58. PERIMETER	Border or boundary
59. PERSISTENT	Refuses to give up or let go; long-lasting
60. PRIED	Separated or moved something with great difficulty
61. PROMINENCE	The condition of being immediately noticeable or recognizable
62. PROSTRATE	Lying flat on the ground in humility or submission
63. RECEDING	Becoming more distant
64. RELENTLESSLY	Steadily; in a way never giving up
65. RELUCTANTLY	Not willingly; with resistance or hesitation
66. RESEMBLANCE	Similarity of likeness with something else
67. RESTITUTION	Compensation for loss or damage
68. RETALIATE	Get revenge; pay back in kind for a wrong-doing
69. REVERENCE	Feeling or attitude of deep respect
70. RIGID	Stiff; inflexible; hard
71. ROUT	An overwhelming defeat
72. SATURATING	Soaking thoroughly and completely
73. SCARCE	Uncommonly or infrequently found or seen
74. SCRIMMAGE	Practice session or informal game
75. SINGED	Burned slightly; scorched
76. SOLEMNLY	Seriously; gravely; in a somber manner
77. SPECTACLE	Public performance or display
78. SUBDUED	Quiet; repressed; controlled
79. TROUNCED	Beat severely
80. UNISON	Corresponding exactly and occurring at the same time
81. UNPRECEDENTED	Never before known, experienced, or done
82. VEERED	Turned or swerved off course
83. VEHEMENTLY	Strongly; violently; with forceful expression of emotion or belief
84. VERGE	On the edge; the point where an action is likely to begin
85. VICIOUS	Ferocious; unpleasantly severe
86. VULNERABLE	Capable of being wounded or hurt
87. WAIVE	Give up a right or claim voluntarily
88. WRATH	Strong, vindictive, or fierce anger

Tangerine Vocabulary Fill In The Blanks 1

_____
_____
_____
_____
_____
_____
_____
_____
_____
_____
_____
_____
_____
_____
_____
_____
_____
_____
_____
_____

1. Subjected to smoke or fumes, usually to exterminate bugs
2. Refuses to give up or let go; long-lasting
3. Extending in the same direction, equally distant at every point
4. Amazement or astonishment
5. Breaking up; deteriorating; falling apart
6. With great concentration or eager attention
7. Very happy or proud; in high spirits
8. Having folds, ridges, and grooves
9. Suddenly or unexpectedly
10. Disliked intensely; scorned; loathed
11. Legally obligated or responsible
12. Surrender or give up as punishment for a crime, error, or offense
13. Main enemy
14. Light, teasing, playful remarks
15. An overwhelming defeat
16. A swell, almost like a bubble, in an artery; if it bursts, it is usually fatal
17. Capable of being wounded or hurt
18. Turned or swerved off course
19. Things that are not within the usual rules or customs
20. Upset or disturbed

Tangerine Vocabulary Fill In The Blanks 1 Answer Key

FUMIGATED	1. Subjected to smoke or fumes, usually to exterminate bugs
PERSISTENT	2. Refuses to give up or let go; long-lasting
PARALLEL	3. Extending in the same direction, equally distant at every point
DISBELIEF	4. Amazement or astonishment
DISINTEGRATING	5. Breaking up; deteriorating; falling apart
INTENTLY	6. With great concentration or eager attention
ELATED	7. Very happy or proud; in high spirits
CORRUGATED	8. Having folds, ridges, and grooves
ABRUPTLY	9. Suddenly or unexpectedly
DESPISED	10. Disliked intensely; scorned; loathed
LIABLE	11. Legally obligated or responsible
FORFEIT	12. Surrender or give up as punishment for a crime, error, or offense
ARCHENEMY	13. Main enemy
BANTER	14. Light, teasing, playful remarks
ROUT	15. An overwhelming defeat
ANEURYSM	16. A swell, almost like a bubble, in an artery; if it bursts, it is usually fatal
VULNERABLE	17. Capable of being wounded or hurt
VEERED	18. Turned or swerved off course
IRREGULARITIES	19. Things that are not within the usual rules or customs
AGITATED	20. Upset or disturbed

Tangerine Vocabulary Fill In The Blanks 2

_____
_____
_____
_____
_____
_____
_____
_____
_____
_____
_____
_____
_____
_____
_____
_____
_____
_____
_____
_____

1. Quiet; repressed; controlled
2. The condition of being immediately noticeable or recognizable
3. One leg on either side of; straddling
4. Becoming more distant
5. Required; bonded
6. Understand
7. Suspend (as a meeting) to or until another place or time
8. Turning or flipping over
9. Ruined or decayed from age, wear, or neglect
10. Written statements made under oath
11. Strangely cruel or monstrous
12. Seriously; gravely; in a somber manner
13. Outstanding events in which a person puts his or her strong points to the best advantage
14. Moving (usually upward or outward) in a rolling, swelling motion
15. Violation; breach
16. Main enemy
17. The science or art of cultivating plants
18. Feeling or attitude of deep respect
19. Not regular or predictable
20. Strong, vindictive, or fierce anger

Tangerine Vocabulary Fill In The Blanks 2 Answer Key

SUBDUED	1. Quiet; repressed; controlled
PROMINENCE	2. The condition of being immediately noticeable or recognizable
ASTRIDE	3. One leg on either side of; straddling
RECEDING	4. Becoming more distant
OBLIGED	5. Required; bonded
COMPREHEND	6. Understand
ADJOURN	7. Suspend (as a meeting) to or until another place or time
CAPSIZING	8. Turning or flipping over
DILAPIDATED	9. Ruined or decayed from age, wear, or neglect
AFFIDAVITS	10. Written statements made under oath
GHOULISH	11. Strangely cruel or monstrous
SOLEMNLY	12. Seriously; gravely; in a somber manner
EXPLOITS	13. Outstanding events in which a person puts his or her strong points to the best advantage
BILLOWING	14. Moving (usually upward or outward) in a rolling, swelling motion
INFRACTION	15. Violation; breach
ARCHENEMY	16. Main enemy
HORTICULTURE	17. The science or art of cultivating plants
REVERENCE	18. Feeling or attitude of deep respect
INCONSISTENT	19. Not regular or predictable
WRATH	20. Strong, vindictive, or fierce anger

Tangerine Vocabulary Fill In The Blanks 3

1. Lying flat on the ground in humility or submission
2. Surrender or give up as punishment for a crime, error, or offense
3. Escort; a group (as of vehicles) traveling together for convenience
4. Compensation for loss or damage
5. With great concentration or eager attention
6. Capable of being wounded or hurt
7. Refuses to give up or let go; long-lasting
8. Something or someone used to lure or mislead another into a trap
9. Twist into a strange shape or expression
10. Threatening or dangerous
11. Worked together willingly and agreeably
12. Suspend (as a meeting) to or until another place or time
13. Stiff; inflexible; hard
14. Feeling or attitude of deep respect
15. Strong, vindictive, or fierce anger
16. Filled with distress, suffering, or torture; worrying in a distressed way
17. Separated or moved something with great difficulty
18. Very small, biting fly
19. Extremely tense or nervous
20. Suddenly or unexpectedly

Tangerine Vocabulary Fill In The Blanks 3 Answer Key

PROSTRATE	1. Lying flat on the ground in humility or submission
FORFEIT	2. Surrender or give up as punishment for a crime, error, or offense
CONVOY	3. Escort; a group (as of vehicles) traveling together for convenience
RESTITUTION	4. Compensation for loss or damage
INTENTLY	5. With great concentration or eager attention
VULNERABLE	6. Capable of being wounded or hurt
PERSISTENT	7. Refuses to give up or let go; long-lasting
DECOY	8. Something or someone used to lure or mislead another into a trap
CONTORT	9. Twist into a strange shape or expression
MENACING	10. Threatening or dangerous
COOPERATED	11. Worked together willingly and agreeably
ADJOURN	12. Suspend (as a meeting) to or until another place or time
RIGID	13. Stiff; inflexible; hard
REVERENCE	14. Feeling or attitude of deep respect
WRATH	15. Strong, vindictive, or fierce anger
AGONIZING	16. Filled with distress, suffering, or torture; worrying in a distressed way
PRIED	17. Separated or moved something with great difficulty
GNAT	18. Very small, biting fly
JITTERY	19. Extremely tense or nervous
ABRUPTLY	20. Suddenly or unexpectedly

Tangerine Vocabulary Fill In The Blanks 4

1. Things that are not within the usual rules or customs
2. Chemical agent used to destroy bacteria
3. Light, teasing, playful remarks
4. Came between to mediate or help
5. An overwhelming defeat
6. Separated or moved something with great difficulty
7. One's own moral or ethical awareness of right and wrong
8. Suspend (as a meeting) to or until another place or time
9. Signal used to prompt an action
10. Never before known, experienced, or done
11. Rise up or swell; bulge; lift
12. Stiff; inflexible; hard
13. Border or boundary
14. Was in deep thought; focused attention on one subject persistently
15. Quickly
16. Soaking thoroughly and completely
17. Bombarding; striking rapidly and repeatedly
18. Ferocious; unpleasantly severe
19. A swell, almost like a bubble, in an artery; if it bursts, it is usually fatal
20. Written statements made under oath

Tangerine Vocabulary Fill In The Blanks 4 Answer Key

IRREGULARITIES	1. Things that are not within the usual rules or customs
DISINFECTANT	2. Chemical agent used to destroy bacteria
BANTER	3. Light, teasing, playful remarks
INTERVENED	4. Came between to mediate or help
ROUT	5. An overwhelming defeat
PRIED	6. Separated or moved something with great difficulty
CONSCIENCE	7. One's own moral or ethical awareness of right and wrong
ADJOURN	8. Suspend (as a meeting) to or until another place or time
CUE	9. Signal used to prompt an action
UNPRECEDENTED	10. Never before known, experienced, or done
HEAVE	11. Rise up or swell; bulge; lift
RIGID	12. Stiff; inflexible; hard
PERIMETER	13. Border or boundary
BROODED	14. Was in deep thought; focused attention on one subject persistently
HASTILY	15. Quickly
SATURATING	16. Soaking thoroughly and completely
PELTING	17. Bombarding; striking rapidly and repeatedly
VICIOUS	18. Ferocious; unpleasantly severe
ANEURYSM	19. A swell, almost like a bubble, in an artery; if it bursts, it is usually fatal
AFFIDAVITS	20. Written statements made under oath

Tangerine Vocabulary Matching 1

___ 1. ADJOURN
___ 2. INCONSISTENT
___ 3. RIGID
___ 4. SUBDUED
___ 5. HASTILY
___ 6. CONVOY
___ 7. ECLIPSE
___ 8. PERIMETER
___ 9. BILLOWING
___ 10. VEHEMENTLY
___ 11. RELUCTANTLY
___ 12. ROUT
___ 13. IMPATIENT
___ 14. VERGE
___ 15. SATURATING
___ 16. BROODED
___ 17. DECOY
___ 18. MENACING
___ 19. HEAVE
___ 20. CORRUGATED
___ 21. RETALIATE
___ 22. DISINFECTANT
___ 23. DILAPIDATED
___ 24. INSOLENTLY
___ 25. VICIOUS

A. Get revenge; pay back in kind for a wrong-doing
B. Stiff; inflexible; hard
C. In a way that is boldly rude or disrespectful
D. Not regular or predictable
E. Wanting to hurry up; not wanting to wait for something to be done or to happen
F. Strongly; violently; with forceful expression of emotion or belief
G. Moving (usually upward or outward) in a rolling, swelling motion
H. Having folds, ridges, and grooves
I. Something or someone used to lure or mislead another into a trap
J. Quiet; repressed; controlled
K. Ferocious; unpleasantly severe
L. The disappearance of the whole or a part of the sun when the moon comes between it and earth
M. An overwhelming defeat
N. Was in deep thought; focused attention on one subject persistently
O. Quickly
P. Ruined or decayed from age, wear, or neglect
Q. On the edge; the point where an action is likely to begin
R. Soaking thoroughly and completely
S. Escort; a group (as of vehicles) traveling together for convenience
T. Not willingly; with resistance or hesitation
U. Suspend (as a meeting) to or until another place or time
V. Threatening or dangerous
W. Chemical agent used to destroy bacteria
X. Rise up or swell; bulge; lift
Y. Border or boundary

Tangerine Vocabulary Matching 1 Answer Key

U - 1. ADJOURN
D - 2. INCONSISTENT
B - 3. RIGID
J - 4. SUBDUED
O - 5. HASTILY
S - 6. CONVOY
L - 7. ECLIPSE
Y - 8. PERIMETER
G - 9. BILLOWING
F - 10. VEHEMENTLY
T - 11. RELUCTANTLY
M - 12. ROUT
E - 13. IMPATIENT
Q - 14. VERGE
R - 15. SATURATING
N - 16. BROODED
I - 17. DECOY
V - 18. MENACING
X - 19. HEAVE
H - 20. CORRUGATED
A - 21. RETALIATE
W - 22. DISINFECTANT
P - 23. DILAPIDATED
C - 24. INSOLENTLY
K - 25. VICIOUS

A. Get revenge; pay back in kind for a wrong-doing
B. Stiff; inflexible; hard
C. In a way that is boldly rude or disrespectful
D. Not regular or predictable
E. Wanting to hurry up; not wanting to wait for something to be done or to happen
F. Strongly; violently; with forceful expression of emotion or belief
G. Moving (usually upward or outward) in a rolling, swelling motion
H. Having folds, ridges, and grooves
I. Something or someone used to lure or mislead another into a trap
J. Quiet; repressed; controlled
K. Ferocious; unpleasantly severe
L. The disappearance of the whole or a part of the sun when the moon comes between it and earth
M. An overwhelming defeat
N. Was in deep thought; focused attention on one subject persistently
O. Quickly
P. Ruined or decayed from age, wear, or neglect
Q. On the edge; the point where an action is likely to begin
R. Soaking thoroughly and completely
S. Escort; a group (as of vehicles) traveling together for convenience
T. Not willingly; with resistance or hesitation
U. Suspend (as a meeting) to or until another place or time
V. Threatening or dangerous
W. Chemical agent used to destroy bacteria
X. Rise up or swell; bulge; lift
Y. Border or boundary

Tangerine Vocabulary Matching 2

___ 1. AFFIDAVITS
___ 2. ARCHENEMY
___ 3. PARALLEL
___ 4. AGONIZING
___ 5. CAPSIZING
___ 6. SOLEMNLY
___ 7. CALISTHENICS
___ 8. INTENTLY
___ 9. TROUNCED
___ 10. CONSCIENCE
___ 11. DILAPIDATED
___ 12. DECOY
___ 13. ECLIPSE
___ 14. CONTORT
___ 15. RETALIATE
___ 16. GNAT
___ 17. NULLIFY
___ 18. DISINTEGRATING
___ 19. PELTING
___ 20. UNPRECEDENTED
___ 21. CONVICTION
___ 22. VEHEMENTLY
___ 23. AGITATED
___ 24. DESPISED
___ 25. INTERVENED

A. Get revenge; pay back in kind for a wrong-doing
B. Written statements made under oath
C. Bombarding; striking rapidly and repeatedly
D. Extending in the same direction, equally distant at every point
E. Ruined or decayed from age, wear, or neglect
F. Exercises to develop muscles
G. Declare something void; invalidate
H. Something or someone used to lure or mislead another into a trap
I. One's own moral or ethical awareness of right and wrong
J. The disappearance of the whole or a part of the sun when the moon comes between it and earth
K. Upset or disturbed
L. Strongly; violently; with forceful expression of emotion or belief
M. Very small, biting fly
N. Breaking up; deteriorating; falling apart
O. Seriously; gravely; in a somber manner
P. Fixed or firm belief
Q. Turning or flipping over
R. Never before known, experienced, or done
S. Disliked intensely; scorned; loathed
T. Came between to mediate or help
U. Beat severely
V. Filled with distress, suffering, or torture; worrying in a distressed way
W. Twist into a strange shape or expression
X. With great concentration or eager attention
Y. Main enemy

Tangerine Vocabulary Matching 2 Answer Key

B - 1. AFFIDAVITS	A. Get revenge; pay back in kind for a wrong-doing
Y - 2. ARCHENEMY	B. Written statements made under oath
D - 3. PARALLEL	C. Bombarding; striking rapidly and repeatedly
V - 4. AGONIZING	D. Extending in the same direction, equally distant at every point
Q - 5. CAPSIZING	E. Ruined or decayed from age, wear, or neglect
O - 6. SOLEMNLY	F. Exercises to develop muscles
F - 7. CALISTHENICS	G. Declare something void; invalidate
X - 8. INTENTLY	H. Something or someone used to lure or mislead another into a trap
U - 9. TROUNCED	I. One's own moral or ethical awareness of right and wrong
I - 10. CONSCIENCE	J. The disappearance of the whole or a part of the sun when the moon comes between it and earth
E - 11. DILAPIDATED	K. Upset or disturbed
H - 12. DECOY	L. Strongly; violently; with forceful expression of emotion or belief
J - 13. ECLIPSE	M. Very small, biting fly
W - 14. CONTORT	N. Breaking up; deteriorating; falling apart
A - 15. RETALIATE	O. Seriously; gravely; in a somber manner
M - 16. GNAT	P. Fixed or firm belief
G - 17. NULLIFY	Q. Turning or flipping over
N - 18. DISINTEGRATING	R. Never before known, experienced, or done
C - 19. PELTING	S. Disliked intensely; scorned; loathed
R - 20. UNPRECEDENTED	T. Came between to mediate or help
P - 21. CONVICTION	U. Beat severely
L - 22. VEHEMENTLY	V. Filled with distress, suffering, or torture; worrying in a distressed way
K - 23. AGITATED	W. Twist into a strange shape or expression
S - 24. DESPISED	X. With great concentration or eager attention
T - 25. INTERVENED	Y. Main enemy

Tangerine Vocabulary Matching 3

___ 1. UNISON
___ 2. AGONIZING
___ 3. INTERVENED
___ 4. MENACING
___ 5. RELUCTANTLY
___ 6. VERGE
___ 7. ARCHENEMY
___ 8. WAIVE
___ 9. CUE
___ 10. SOLEMNLY
___ 11. CONTORT
___ 12. JITTERY
___ 13. RETALIATE
___ 14. DISINTEGRATING
___ 15. ELATED
___ 16. DISBELIEF
___ 17. DILAPIDATED
___ 18. BROODED
___ 19. SPECTACLE
___ 20. WRATH
___ 21. COOPERATED
___ 22. VICIOUS
___ 23. GHOULISH
___ 24. PRIED
___ 25. COMPREHEND

A. Filled with distress, suffering, or torture; worrying in a distressed way
B. Signal used to prompt an action
C. Strangely cruel or monstrous
D. Main enemy
E. Threatening or dangerous
F. Ferocious; unpleasantly severe
G. Was in deep thought; focused attention on one subject persistently
H. Get revenge; pay back in kind for a wrong-doing
I. Corresponding exactly and occurring at the same time
J. Public performance or display
K. Came between to mediate or help
L. Understand
M. Extremely tense or nervous
N. Not willingly; with resistance or hesitation
O. Give up a right or claim voluntarily
P. Very happy or proud; in high spirits
Q. Worked together willingly and agreeably
R. On the edge; the point where an action is likely to begin
S. Separated or moved something with great difficulty
T. Twist into a strange shape or expression
U. Ruined or decayed from age, wear, or neglect
V. Strong, vindictive, or fierce anger
W. Amazement or astonishment
X. Breaking up; deteriorating; falling apart
Y. Seriously; gravely; in a somber manner

Tangerine Vocabulary Matching 3 Answer Key

I - 1. UNISON
A - 2. AGONIZING
K - 3. INTERVENED
E - 4. MENACING
N - 5. RELUCTANTLY
R - 6. VERGE
D - 7. ARCHENEMY
O - 8. WAIVE
B - 9. CUE
Y - 10. SOLEMNLY
T - 11. CONTORT
M - 12. JITTERY
H - 13. RETALIATE
X - 14. DISINTEGRATING
P - 15. ELATED
W - 16. DISBELIEF
U - 17. DILAPIDATED
G - 18. BROODED
J - 19. SPECTACLE
V - 20. WRATH
Q - 21. COOPERATED
F - 22. VICIOUS
C - 23. GHOULISH
S - 24. PRIED
L - 25. COMPREHEND

A. Filled with distress, suffering, or torture; worrying in a distressed way
B. Signal used to prompt an action
C. Strangely cruel or monstrous
D. Main enemy
E. Threatening or dangerous
F. Ferocious; unpleasantly severe
G. Was in deep thought; focused attention on one subject persistently
H. Get revenge; pay back in kind for a wrong-doing
I. Corresponding exactly and occurring at the same time
J. Public performance or display
K. Came between to mediate or help
L. Understand
M. Extremely tense or nervous
N. Not willingly; with resistance or hesitation
O. Give up a right or claim voluntarily
P. Very happy or proud; in high spirits
Q. Worked together willingly and agreeably
R. On the edge; the point where an action is likely to begin
S. Separated or moved something with great difficulty
T. Twist into a strange shape or expression
U. Ruined or decayed from age, wear, or neglect
V. Strong, vindictive, or fierce anger
W. Amazement or astonishment
X. Breaking up; deteriorating; falling apart
Y. Seriously; gravely; in a somber manner

Tangerine Vocabulary Matching 4

___ 1. ELATED
___ 2. CONSCIENCE
___ 3. DECOY
___ 4. BANTER
___ 5. IMPATIENT
___ 6. DISINTEGRATING
___ 7. TROUNCED
___ 8. OVATION
___ 9. PROMINENCE
___ 10. HASTILY
___ 11. DWELL
___ 12. CONSTITUTES
___ 13. PROSTRATE
___ 14. OMINOUSLY
___ 15. LIABLE
___ 16. VEHEMENTLY
___ 17. HEAVE
___ 18. AGITATED
___ 19. RELUCTANTLY
___ 20. CONVOY
___ 21. COMPREHEND
___ 22. RESTITUTION
___ 23. AGONIZING
___ 24. DILAPIDATED
___ 25. PERIMETER

A. Filled with distress, suffering, or torture; worrying in a distressed way
B. Understand
C. Something or someone used to lure or mislead another into a trap
D. Makes the elements or parts of
E. Quickly
F. One's own moral or ethical awareness of right and wrong
G. Very happy or proud; in high spirits
H. Compensation for loss or damage
I. Wanting to hurry up; not wanting to wait for something to be done or to happen
J. Upset or disturbed
K. Focus one's attention on (usually a thought) for an extended period of time
L. Breaking up; deteriorating; falling apart
M. In a threatening way
N. Ruined or decayed from age, wear, or neglect
O. Enthusiastic, prolonged applause
P. The condition of being immediately noticeable or recognizable
Q. Lying flat on the ground in humility or submission
R. Legally obligated or responsible
S. Beat severely
T. Rise up or swell; bulge; lift
U. Escort; a group (as of vehicles) traveling together for convenience
V. Light, teasing, playful remarks
W. Strongly; violently; with forceful expression of emotion or belief
X. Not willingly; with resistance or hesitation
Y. Border or boundary

Tangerine Vocabulary Matching 4 Answer Key

G - 1. ELATED	A.	Filled with distress, suffering, or torture; worrying in a distressed way
F - 2. CONSCIENCE	B.	Understand
C - 3. DECOY	C.	Something or someone used to lure or mislead another into a trap
V - 4. BANTER	D.	Makes the elements or parts of
I - 5. IMPATIENT	E.	Quickly
L - 6. DISINTEGRATING	F.	One's own moral or ethical awareness of right and wrong
S - 7. TROUNCED	G.	Very happy or proud; in high spirits
O - 8. OVATION	H.	Compensation for loss or damage
P - 9. PROMINENCE	I.	Wanting to hurry up; not wanting to wait for something to be done or to happen
E - 10. HASTILY	J.	Upset or disturbed
K - 11. DWELL	K.	Focus one's attention on (usually a thought) for an extended period of time
D - 12. CONSTITUTES	L.	Breaking up; deteriorating; falling apart
Q - 13. PROSTRATE	M.	In a threatening way
M - 14. OMINOUSLY	N.	Ruined or decayed from age, wear, or neglect
R - 15. LIABLE	O.	Enthusiastic, prolonged applause
W - 16. VEHEMENTLY	P.	The condition of being immediately noticeable or recognizable
T - 17. HEAVE	Q.	Lying flat on the ground in humility or submission
J - 18. AGITATED	R.	Legally obligated or responsible
X - 19. RELUCTANTLY	S.	Beat severely
U - 20. CONVOY	T.	Rise up or swell; bulge; lift
B - 21. COMPREHEND	U.	Escort; a group (as of vehicles) traveling together for convenience
H - 22. RESTITUTION	V.	Light, teasing, playful remarks
A - 23. AGONIZING	W.	Strongly; violently; with forceful expression of emotion or belief
N - 24. DILAPIDATED	X.	Not willingly; with resistance or hesitation
Y - 25. PERIMETER	Y.	Border or boundary

Tangerine Vocabulary Magic Squares 1

Match the definition with the vocabulary word. Put your answers in the magic squares below. When your answers are correct, all columns and rows will add to the same number.

A. VERGE
B. MENACING
C. SCARCE
D. INSOLENTLY
E. COMPREHEND
F. DWELL
G. REVERENCE
H. OVATION
I. WAIVE
J. SOLEMNLY
K. CALISTHENICS
L. CONSTITUTES
M. RECEDING
N. PERSISTENT
O. INCONSISTENT
P. LIABLE

1. Not regular or predictable
2. In a way that is boldly rude or disrespectful
3. Seriously; gravely; in a somber manner
4. Understand
5. Give up a right or claim voluntarily
6. Focus one's attention on (usually a thought) for an extended period of time
7. Legally obligated or responsible
8. Uncommonly or infrequently found or seen
9. Enthusiastic, prolonged applause
10. Exercises to develop muscles
11. On the edge; the point where an action is likely to begin
12. Refuses to give up or let go; long-lasting
13. Threatening or dangerous
14. Becoming more distant
15. Feeling or attitude of deep respect
16. Makes the elements or parts of

A=	B=	C=	D=
E=	F=	G=	H=
I=	J=	K=	L=
M=	N=	O=	P=

Tangerine Vocabulary Magic Squares 1 Answer Key

Match the definition with the vocabulary word. Put your answers in the magic squares below. When your answers are correct, all columns and rows will add to the same number.

A. VERGE
B. MENACING
C. SCARCE
D. INSOLENTLY
E. COMPREHEND
F. DWELL
G. REVERENCE
H. OVATION
I. WAIVE
J. SOLEMNLY
K. CALISTHENICS
L. CONSTITUTES
M. RECEDING
N. PERSISTENT
O. INCONSISTENT
P. LIABLE

1. Not regular or predictable
2. In a way that is boldly rude or disrespectful
3. Seriously; gravely; in a somber manner
4. Understand
5. Give up a right or claim voluntarily
6. Focus one's attention on (usually a thought) for an extended period of time
7. Legally obligated or responsible
8. Uncommonly or infrequently found or seen
9. Enthusiastic, prolonged applause
10. Exercises to develop muscles
11. On the edge; the point where an action is likely to begin
12. Refuses to give up or let go; long-lasting
13. Threatening or dangerous
14. Becoming more distant
15. Feeling or attitude of deep respect
16. Makes the elements or parts of

A=11	B=13	C=8	D=2
E=4	F=6	G=15	H=9
I=5	J=3	K=10	L=16
M=14	N=12	O=1	P=7

Tangerine Vocabulary Magic Squares 2

Match the definition with the vocabulary word. Put your answers in the magic squares below. When your answers are correct, all columns and rows will add to the same number.

A. PRIED
B. DESPISED
C. HEAVE
D. INTERVENED
E. CUE
F. RESEMBLANCE
G. JITTERY
H. RELENTLESSLY
I. DECOY
J. OBLIGED
K. SUBDUED
L. CAPSIZING
M. BANTER
N. INTENTLY
O. REVERENCE
P. ABRUPTLY

1. Disliked intensely; scorned; loathed
2. Extremely tense or nervous
3. Quiet; repressed; controlled
4. With great concentration or eager attention
5. Light, teasing, playful remarks
6. Turning or flipping over
7. Steadily; in a way never giving up
8. Separated or moved something with great difficulty
9. Suddenly or unexpectedly
10. Something or someone used to lure or mislead another into a trap
11. Signal used to prompt an action
12. Came between to mediate or help
13. Rise up or swell; bulge; lift
14. Similarity of likeness with something else
15. Required; bonded
16. Feeling or attitude of deep respect

A=	B=	C=	D=
E=	F=	G=	H=
I=	J=	K=	L=
M=	N=	O=	P=

Tangerine Vocabulary Magic Squares 2 Answer Key

Match the definition with the vocabulary word. Put your answers in the magic squares below. When your answers are correct, all columns and rows will add to the same number.

A. PRIED
B. DESPISED
C. HEAVE
D. INTERVENED
E. CUE
F. RESEMBLANCE
G. JITTERY
H. RELENTLESSLY
I. DECOY
J. OBLIGED
K. SUBDUED
L. CAPSIZING
M. BANTER
N. INTENTLY
O. REVERENCE
P. ABRUPTLY

1. Disliked intensely; scorned; loathed
2. Extremely tense or nervous
3. Quiet; repressed; controlled
4. With great concentration or eager attention
5. Light, teasing, playful remarks
6. Turning or flipping over
7. Steadily; in a way never giving up
8. Separated or moved something with great difficulty
9. Suddenly or unexpectedly
10. Something or someone used to lure or mislead another into a trap
11. Signal used to prompt an action
12. Came between to mediate or help
13. Rise up or swell; bulge; lift
14. Similarity of likeness with something else
15. Required; bonded
16. Feeling or attitude of deep respect

A=8	B=1	C=13	D=12
E=11	F=14	G=2	H=7
I=10	J=15	K=3	L=6
M=5	N=4	O=16	P=9

Tangerine Vocabulary Magic Squares 3

Match the definition with the vocabulary word. Put your answers in the magic squares below. When your answers are correct, all columns and rows will add to the same number.

A. OMINOUSLY
B. CAPSIZING
C. GHOULISH
D. GNAT
E. VEHEMENTLY
F. VERGE
G. ARCHENEMY
H. JEERING
I. LIABLE
J. ADJOURN
K. FUMIGATED
L. CONTORT
M. WRATH
N. DILAPIDATED
O. CORRUGATED
P. PARALLEL

1. Mocking, taunting, or verbally abusing
2. In a threatening way
3. Turning or flipping over
4. Main enemy
5. Suspend (as a meeting) to or until another place or time
6. Having folds, ridges, and grooves
7. Extending in the same direction, equally distant at every point
8. Legally obligated or responsible
9. Subjected to smoke or fumes, usually to exterminate bugs
10. Ruined or decayed from age, wear, or neglect
11. Strong, vindictive, or fierce anger
12. Twist into a strange shape or expression
13. Strongly; violently; with forceful expression of emotion or belief
14. Very small, biting fly
15. Strangely cruel or monstrous
16. On the edge; the point where an action is likely to begin

A=	B=	C=	D=
E=	F=	G=	H=
I=	J=	K=	L=
M=	N=	O=	P=

Tangerine Vocabulary Magic Squares 3 Answer Key

Match the definition with the vocabulary word. Put your answers in the magic squares below. When your answers are correct, all columns and rows will add to the same number.

A. OMINOUSLY
B. CAPSIZING
C. GHOULISH
D. GNAT
E. VEHEMENTLY
F. VERGE
G. ARCHENEMY
H. JEERING
I. LIABLE
J. ADJOURN
K. FUMIGATED
L. CONTORT
M. WRATH
N. DILAPIDATED
O. CORRUGATED
P. PARALLEL

1. Mocking, taunting, or verbally abusing
2. In a threatening way
3. Turning or flipping over
4. Main enemy
5. Suspend (as a meeting) to or until another place or time
6. Having folds, ridges, and grooves
7. Extending in the same direction, equally distant at every point
8. Legally obligated or responsible
9. Subjected to smoke or fumes, usually to exterminate bugs
10. Ruined or decayed from age, wear, or neglect
11. Strong, vindictive, or fierce anger
12. Twist into a strange shape or expression
13. Strongly; violently; with forceful expression of emotion or belief
14. Very small, biting fly
15. Strangely cruel or monstrous
16. On the edge; the point where an action is likely to begin

A=2	B=3	C=15	D=14
E=13	F=16	G=4	H=1
I=8	J=5	K=9	L=12
M=11	N=10	O=6	P=7

Tangerine Vocabulary Magic Squares 4

Match the definition with the vocabulary word. Put your answers in the magic squares below. When your answers are correct, all columns and rows will add to the same number.

A. HORTICULTURE
B. VEERED
C. DISCLOSURE
D. IMPATIENT
E. DILAPIDATED
F. AFFIDAVITS
G. CALISTHENICS
H. PELTING
I. LIABLE
J. INCONSISTENT
K. OBLIGED
L. DWELL
M. RESTITUTION
N. CONVICTION
O. WAIVE
P. CORRUGATED

1. Written statements made under oath
2. Legally obligated or responsible
3. Give up a right or claim voluntarily
4. Wanting to hurry up; not wanting to wait for something to be done or to happen
5. Compensation for loss or damage
6. Turned or swerved off course
7. Bombarding; striking rapidly and repeatedly
8. Required; bonded
9. Making facts and details evident and clear
10. Having folds, ridges, and grooves
11. Not regular or predictable
12. Ruined or decayed from age, wear, or neglect
13. Focus one's attention on (usually a thought) for an extended period of time
14. Exercises to develop muscles
15. The science or art of cultivating plants
16. Fixed or firm belief

A=	B=	C=	D=
E=	F=	G=	H=
I=	J=	K=	L=
M=	N=	O=	P=

Tangerine Vocabulary Magic Squares 4 Answer Key

Match the definition with the vocabulary word. Put your answers in the magic squares below. When your answers are correct, all columns and rows will add to the same number.

A. HORTICULTURE
B. VEERED
C. DISCLOSURE
D. IMPATIENT
E. DILAPIDATED
F. AFFIDAVITS
G. CALISTHENICS
H. PELTING
I. LIABLE
J. INCONSISTENT
K. OBLIGED
L. DWELL
M. RESTITUTION
N. CONVICTION
O. WAIVE
P. CORRUGATED

1. Written statements made under oath
2. Legally obligated or responsible
3. Give up a right or claim voluntarily
4. Wanting to hurry up; not wanting to wait for something to be done or to happen
5. Compensation for loss or damage
6. Turned or swerved off course
7. Bombarding; striking rapidly and repeatedly
8. Required; bonded
9. Making facts and details evident and clear
10. Having folds, ridges, and grooves
11. Not regular or predictable
12. Ruined or decayed from age, wear, or neglect
13. Focus one's attention on (usually a thought) for an extended period of time
14. Exercises to develop muscles
15. The science or art of cultivating plants
16. Fixed or firm belief

A=15	B=6	C=9	D=4
E=12	F=1	G=14	H=7
I=2	J=11	K=8	L=13
M=5	N=16	O=3	P=10

Tangerine Vocabulary Juggle Letters 1

1. LLWDE = 1. _____
   Focus one's attention on (usually a thought) for an extended period of time

2. NELURLVBAE = 2. _____
   Capable of being wounded or hurt

3. ITNRUESTOIT = 3. _____
   Compensation for loss or damage

4. RUETGIARIIESRL = 4. _____
   Things that are not within the usual rules or customs

5. ESGIDN = 5. _____
   Burned slightly; scorched

6. SLBEAMCENRE = 6. _____
   Similarity of likeness with something else

7. SUYAENRM = 7. _____
   A swell, almost like a bubble, in an artery; if it bursts, it is usually fatal

8. ECERIGND = 8. _____
   Becoming more distant

9. SHUOIGHL = 9. _____
   Strangely cruel or monstrous

10. SLNCSACITIHE =10. _____
    Exercises to develop muscles

11. MEREPTIRE =11. _____
    Border or boundary

12. ESSDIPDE =12. _____
    Disliked intensely; scorned; loathed

13. ENECEERVR =13. _____
    Feeling or attitude of deep respect

14. ETMPAINIT =14. _____
    Wanting to hurry up; not wanting to wait for something to be done or to happen

Tangerine Vocabulary Juggle Letters 1 Answer Key

1. LLWDE = 1. DWELL
   Focus one's attention on (usually a thought) for an extended period of time

2. NELURLVBAE = 2. VULNERABLE
   Capable of being wounded or hurt

3. ITNRUESTOIT = 3. RESTITUTION
   Compensation for loss or damage

4. RUETGIARIIESRL = 4. IRREGULARITIES
   Things that are not within the usual rules or customs

5. ESGIDN = 5. SINGED
   Burned slightly; scorched

6. SLBEAMCENRE = 6. RESEMBLANCE
   Similarity of likeness with something else

7. SUYAENRM = 7. ANEURYSM
   A swell, almost like a bubble, in an artery; if it bursts, it is usually fatal

8. ECERIGND = 8. RECEDING
   Becoming more distant

9. SHUOIGHL = 9. GHOULISH
   Strangely cruel or monstrous

10. SLNCSACITIHE =10. CALISTHENICS
    Exercises to develop muscles

11. MEREPTIRE =11. PERIMETER
    Border or boundary

12. ESSDIPDE =12. DESPISED
    Disliked intensely; scorned; loathed

13. ENECEERVR =13. REVERENCE
    Feeling or attitude of deep respect

14. ETMPAINIT =14. IMPATIENT
    Wanting to hurry up; not wanting to wait for something to be done or to happen

Copyrighted

Tangerine Vocabulary Juggle Letters 2

1. AENBTR = 1. _____
Light, teasing, playful remarks

2. RETOOECADP = 2. _____
Worked together willingly and agreeably

3. LGSHHUOI = 3. _____
Strangely cruel or monstrous

4. OSMYLENL = 4. _____
Seriously; gravely; in a somber manner

5. YRAUBPLT = 5. _____
Suddenly or unexpectedly

6. REIFFTO = 6. _____
Surrender or give up as punishment for a crime, error, or offense

7. TEERREMPI = 7. _____
Border or boundary

8. HARTW = 8. _____
Strong, vindictive, or fierce anger

9. PNEDMEROHC = 9. _____
Understand

10. TISLEPXO =10. _____
Outstanding events in which a person puts his or her strong points to the best advantage

11. SRSDULEOIC =11. _____
Making facts and details evident and clear

12. VAIWE =12. _____
Give up a right or claim voluntarily

13. TNEHMEEYLV =13. _____
Strongly; violently; with forceful expression of emotion or belief

14. LLLPEARA =14. _____
Extending in the same direction, equally distant at every point

Tangerine Vocabulary Juggle Letters 2 Answer Key

1. AENBTR = 1. BANTER
   Light, teasing, playful remarks

2. RETOOECADP = 2. COOPERATED
   Worked together willingly and agreeably

3. LGSHHUOI = 3. GHOULISH
   Strangely cruel or monstrous

4. OSMYLENL = 4. SOLEMNLY
   Seriously; gravely; in a somber manner

5. YRAUBPLT = 5. ABRUPTLY
   Suddenly or unexpectedly

6. REIFFTO = 6. FORFEIT
   Surrender or give up as punishment for a crime, error, or offense

7. TEERREMPI = 7. PERIMETER
   Border or boundary

8. HARTW = 8. WRATH
   Strong, vindictive, or fierce anger

9. PNEDMEROHC = 9. COMPREHEND
   Understand

10. TISLEPXO = 10. EXPLOITS
    Outstanding events in which a person puts his or her strong points to the best advantage

11. SRSDULEOIC = 11. DISCLOSURE
    Making facts and details evident and clear

12. VAIWE = 12. WAIVE
    Give up a right or claim voluntarily

13. TNEHMEEYLV = 13. VEHEMENTLY
    Strongly; violently; with forceful expression of emotion or belief

14. LLLPEARA = 14. PARALLEL
    Extending in the same direction, equally distant at every point

Tangerine Vocabulary Juggle Letters 3

1. TEUITSORNIT = 1. _____
   Compensation for loss or damage

2. CEODY = 2. _____
   Something or someone used to lure or mislead another into a trap

3. EADPITLDIDA = 3. _____
   Ruined or decayed from age, wear, or neglect

4. TDNDPNREEEUCE = 4. _____
   Never before known, experienced, or done

5. EIETRPRME = 5. _____
   Border or boundary

6. NRFINACTIO = 6. _____
   Violation; breach

7. ONUINS = 7. _____
   Corresponding exactly and occurring at the same time

8. DFFVTSAIAI = 8. _____
   Written statements made under oath

9. RNPDEHCMOE = 9. _____
   Understand

10. GRJEEIN = 10. _____
    Mocking, taunting, or verbally abusing

11. REIIATLGSRIURE = 11. _____
    Things that are not within the usual rules or customs

12. LRELPALA = 12. _____
    Extending in the same direction, equally distant at every point

13. EOMYLNLS = 13. _____
    Seriously; gravely; in a somber manner

14. MAEGDFTIU = 14. _____
    Subjected to smoke or fumes, usually to exterminate bugs

Tangerine Vocabulary Juggle Letters 3 Answer Key

1. TEUITSORNIT = 1. RESTITUTION
Compensation for loss or damage

2. CEODY = 2. DECOY
Something or someone used to lure or mislead another into a trap

3. EADPITLDIDA = 3. DILAPIDATED
Ruined or decayed from age, wear, or neglect

4. TDNDPNREEEUCE = 4. UNPRECEDENTED
Never before known, experienced, or done

5. EIETRPRME = 5. PERIMETER
Border or boundary

6. NRFINACTIO = 6. INFRACTION
Violation; breach

7. ONUINS = 7. UNISON
Corresponding exactly and occurring at the same time

8. DFFVTSAIAI = 8. AFFIDAVITS
Written statements made under oath

9. RNPDEHCMOE = 9. COMPREHEND
Understand

10. GRJEEIN = 10. JEERING
Mocking, taunting, or verbally abusing

11. REIIATLGSRIURE = 11. IRREGULARITIES
Things that are not within the usual rules or customs

12. LRELPALA = 12. PARALLEL
Extending in the same direction, equally distant at every point

13. EOMYLNLS = 13. SOLEMNLY
Seriously; gravely; in a somber manner

14. MAEGDFTIU = 14. FUMIGATED
Subjected to smoke or fumes, usually to exterminate bugs

Tangerine Vocabulary Juggle Letters 4

1. NIOOATV = 1. _____
   Enthusiastic, prolonged applause

2. HYEVNTEELM = 2. _____
   Strongly; violently; with forceful expression of emotion or belief

3. TXPLOEIS = 3. _____
   Outstanding events in which a person puts his or her strong points to the best advantage

4. YODEC = 4. _____
   Something or someone used to lure or mislead another into a trap

5. EHAEV = 5. _____
   Rise up or swell; bulge; lift

6. AEVWI = 6. _____
   Give up a right or claim voluntarily

7. YLHTAIS = 7. _____
   Quickly

8. ONINGAZIG = 8. _____
   Filled with distress, suffering, or torture; worrying in a distressed way

9. IILGLNOBW = 9. _____
   Moving (usually upward or outward) in a rolling, swelling motion

10. NSOILYNLET =10. _____
    In a way that is boldly rude or disrespectful

11. TDLEAIDAIPD =11. _____
    Ruined or decayed from age, wear, or neglect

12. DTAEIRS =12. _____
    One leg on either side of; straddling

13. NANCMEIG =13. _____
    Threatening or dangerous

14. ETTIUSSNOCT =14. _____
    Makes the elements or parts of

Tangerine Vocabulary Juggle Letters 4 Answer Key

1. NIOOATV = 1. OVATION
   Enthusiastic, prolonged applause

2. HYEVNTEELM = 2. VEHEMENTLY
   Strongly; violently; with forceful expression of emotion or belief

3. TXPLOEIS = 3. EXPLOITS
   Outstanding events in which a person puts his or her strong points to the best advantage

4. YODEC = 4. DECOY
   Something or someone used to lure or mislead another into a trap

5. EHAEV = 5. HEAVE
   Rise up or swell; bulge; lift

6. AEVWI = 6. WAIVE
   Give up a right or claim voluntarily

7. YLHTAIS = 7. HASTILY
   Quickly

8. ONINGAZIG = 8. AGONIZING
   Filled with distress, suffering, or torture; worrying in a distressed way

9. IILGLNOBW = 9. BILLOWING
   Moving (usually upward or outward) in a rolling, swelling motion

10. NSOILYNLET =10. INSOLENTLY
    In a way that is boldly rude or disrespectful

11. TDLEAIDAIPD =11. DILAPIDATED
    Ruined or decayed from age, wear, or neglect

12. DTAEIRS =12. ASTRIDE
    One leg on either side of; straddling

13. NANCMEIG =13. MENACING
    Threatening or dangerous

14. ETTIUSSNOCT =14. CONSTITUTES
    Makes the elements or parts of

Tangerine Vocabulary Word Search 1

```
D I S I N F E C T A N T D B W R A T H G
E N A K A S T R I D E E W G R B Q Y V Q
U T T G N I R E E J X L E A Z O R P E L
D E U R W D B V B O V B L N T E O F R L
B N R X G K A Q T U Y A L E L G B D G D
U T A M N Y N H O R T I C U L T U R E H
S L T L O Y T T A N S L C R R W V T T D
Q Y I V N T E B Q J X T N Y M Y A G R R
T A N G S C R I M M A G E S Q T C N O D
T O G G Y U O E Y N L G E M I P O I U B
C Z Q X P H U D T Y H T O G B I D C N D
E L A T E D T L D A U S A N T K E A C R
J L L G E K Y E S T L Z C U I S S N E R
I Y X I D W G T I N D I T A P Z P E D L
T Y R I L I I T O E E I A I R V I M F W
T P G S L L S S G U T H L T T C S N Y D
E I Q B Y N I N C S T C D P E G E H G K
R C O W O N I L E D E C O Y V S D H W W
Y W Q C U S N R Z H E A V E E R E D X T
```

A swell, almost like a bubble, in an artery; if it bursts, it is usually fatal (8)
An overwhelming defeat (4)
Beat severely (8)
Burned slightly; scorched (6)
Chemical agent used to destroy bacteria (12)
Compensation for loss or damage (11)
Corresponding exactly and occurring at the same time (6)
Disliked intensely; scorned; loathed (8)
Escort; a group (as of vehicles) traveling together for convenience (6)
Extremely tense or nervous (7)
Filled with distress, suffering, or torture; worrying in a distressed way (9)
Focus one's attention on (usually a thought) for an extended period of time (5)
Get revenge; pay back in kind for a wrong-doing (9)
Legally obligated or responsible (6)
Light, teasing, playful remarks (6)
Makes the elements or parts of (11)
Mocking, taunting, or verbally abusing (7)
Not willingly; with resistance or hesitation (11)
On the edge; the point where an action is likely to begin (5)
One leg on either side of; straddling (7)
Practice session or informal game (9)
Quickly (7)
Quiet; repressed; controlled (7)
Required; bonded (7)
Rise up or swell; bulge; lift (5)
Separated or moved something with great difficulty (5)
Signal used to prompt an action (3)
Soaking thoroughly and completely (10)
Something or someone used to lure or mislead another into a trap (5)
Stiff; inflexible; hard (5)
Strong, vindictive, or fierce anger (5)
Suddenly or unexpectedly (8)
Suspend (as a meeting) to or until another place or time (7)
The disappearance of the whole or a part of the sun when the moon comes between it and earth (7)
The science or art of cultivating plants (12)
Threatening or dangerous (8)
Turned or swerved off course (6)
Uncommonly or infrequently found or seen (6)
Upset or disturbed (8)
Very happy or proud; in high spirits (6)
Very small, biting fly (4)
Was in deep thought; focused attention on one subject persistently (7)
With great concentration or eager attention (8)

Tangerine Vocabulary Word Search 1 Answer Key

```
D I S   I N F E C T A N T D B W R A T H
E N A   A S T R I D E E W   R       V
U T T G N I R E E J   L E A   O R   E
D E U       B     O   B L N   E O   R
B N R       A     U   A L E       D G D
U T A   Y N H O R T I C U L T U R E
S L T   O   T   A N   L C R       T T D
  Y I V     E B       T Y     A   G R
T A N G S C R I M M A G E S   T   N O
    O G     U O E     N G E M   I   U
C       P   U   T   H T O G   I D C N
E L A T E D T L D A U S A N T   E A C
J   L   E   Y E S T   C U I S S P N E
I   Y   I D G T I N D I T A P Z P E D
T       R   I I T O E E I A I R   I M
T P G     L L S S G U T   L T   C S N
E I     B Y N I N C S   C     E   E G
R   O   O N I   E D E C O Y     D
Y       C U S   R   H E A V E E R E D
```

A swell, almost like a bubble, in an artery; if it bursts, it is usually fatal (8)
An overwhelming defeat (4)
Beat severely (8)
Burned slightly; scorched (6)
Chemical agent used to destroy bacteria (12)
Compensation for loss or damage (11)
Corresponding exactly and occurring at the same time (6)
Disliked intensely; scorned; loathed (8)
Escort; a group (as of vehicles) traveling together for convenience (6)
Extremely tense or nervous (7)
Filled with distress, suffering, or torture; worrying in a distressed way (9)
Focus one's attention on (usually a thought) for an extended period of time (5)
Get revenge; pay back in kind for a wrong-doing (9)
Legally obligated or responsible (6)
Light, teasing, playful remarks (6)
Makes the elements or parts of (11)
Mocking, taunting, or verbally abusing (7)
Not willingly; with resistance or hesitation (11)
On the edge; the point where an action is likely to begin (5)
One leg on either side of; straddling (7)
Practice session or informal game (9)
Quickly (7)

Quiet; repressed; controlled (7)
Required; bonded (7)
Rise up or swell; bulge; lift (5)
Separated or moved something with great difficulty (5)
Signal used to prompt an action (3)
Soaking thoroughly and completely (10)
Something or someone used to lure or mislead another into a trap (5)
Stiff; inflexible; hard (5)
Strong, vindictive, or fierce anger (5)
Suddenly or unexpectedly (8)
Suspend (as a meeting) to or until another place or time (7)
The disappearance of the whole or a part of the sun when the moon comes between it and earth (7)
The science or art of cultivating plants (12)
Threatening or dangerous (8)
Turned or swerved off course (6)
Uncommonly or infrequently found or seen (6)
Upset or disturbed (8)
Very happy or proud; in high spirits (6)
Very small, biting fly (4)
Was in deep thought; focused attention on one subject persistently (7)
With great concentration or eager attention (8)

Tangerine Vocabulary Word Search 2

```
S A T U R A T I N G S U B D U E D W T Z
C Q G O H V X Z Z P O F N V G E H R H Q
A C U I M Q Z X E Z L K H I T A O A G F
R T M L T F B C Q Z E H T A S T G T C S
C T S I R A T G Y G M H L T N O I H A K
E R Y A R A T O R A N E I O R Q N D F Y
D I R B C P V E R R L L C D C F S R F S
T N U L M N V C D L Y S H E Y V O E I B
N T E E O T H A E H P J M G R I L C D C
A E N C M E Q G S W X E Q N E C E A Y
T N A N N Q A G Q T N J R I T I N D V J
C T F E N M P N N A R F A S T O T I I M
E L M N M D K O C A E I O D I U L N T F
F Y D I L A P I D A T E D R J S Y G S Q
N B R M L H N T E H N U E E F O T L Z J
I C G O J G L A I E A C R V C E U E X R
S S D R Z M G V R A B S E I T O I R N M
I B T P F W M O P V G N E A J P Y T N T
D W E L L G N I R E E J V W R I G I D W
```

A swell, almost like a bubble, in an artery; if it bursts, it is usually fatal (8)
An overwhelming defeat (4)
Becoming more distant (8)
Burned slightly; scorched (6)
Chemical agent used to destroy bacteria (12)
Corresponding exactly and occurring at the same time (6)
Enthusiastic, prolonged applause (7)
Escort; a group (as of vehicles) traveling together for convenience (6)
Extremely tense or nervous (7)
Ferocious; unpleasantly severe (7)
Focus one's attention on (usually a thought) for an extended period of time (5)
Give up a right or claim voluntarily (5)
In a way that is boldly rude or disrespectful (10)
Legally obligated or responsible (6)
Light, teasing, playful remarks (6)
Main enemy (9)
Mocking, taunting, or verbally abusing (7)
On the edge; the point where an action is likely to begin (5)
One leg on either side of; straddling (7)
Practice session or informal game (9)
Public performance or display (9)
Quickly (7)
Quiet; repressed; controlled (7)

Refuses to give up or let go; long-lasting (10)
Rise up or swell; bulge; lift (5)
Ruined or decayed from age, wear, or neglect (11)
Separated or moved something with great difficulty (5)
Seriously; gravely; in a somber manner (8)
Signal used to prompt an action (3)
Soaking thoroughly and completely (10)
Something or someone used to lure or mislead another into a trap (5)
Stiff; inflexible; hard (5)
Strong, vindictive, or fierce anger (5)
Surrender or give up as punishment for a crime, error, or offense (7)
Suspend (as a meeting) to or until another place or time (7)
The condition of being immediately noticeable or recognizable (10)
Threatening or dangerous (8)
Turned or swerved off course (6)
Twist into a strange shape or expression (7)
Uncommonly or infrequently found or seen (6)
Upset or disturbed (8)
Very happy or proud; in high spirits (6)
Very small, biting fly (4)
With great concentration or eager attention (8)
Written statements made under oath (10)

Tangerine Vocabulary Word Search 2 Answer Key

```
S A T U R A T I N G S U B D U E D W T
C   G O           P   O   N     E H R
A   U I         E     L       I T A O A
R T M L T     C       E       A S T   A
C   S I   A T   Y G M     L   T N O I H A
E   Y A   A T O R A N E I O     N   F
    I R B C   V E R   L L C D     S R E I
T N U L   N V C D     Y       E Y V O E D
N T E E O   H A E       P   M G R I L C D
A E N C   E   G S         E   N E C E E A
T N A N   N   A G     T N     R I T I N D V
C T   E     M   N N A R F   A S T O I I
E L M N M     O C A E I   O D I U L N T
F Y D I   L A P I D A T E D R J S Y G S
N   R M     N T E H N U E E F O T
I C   O   G   A I E A C R V C E U E
S     R       V R A B   E I     O I R N
I     P       O P V     E A     Y T N T
D W E L L G N I R E E J V W R I G I D
```

A swell, almost like a bubble, in an artery; if it bursts, it is usually fatal (8)
An overwhelming defeat (4)
Becoming more distant (8)
Burned slightly; scorched (6)
Chemical agent used to destroy bacteria (12)
Corresponding exactly and occurring at the same time (6)
Enthusiastic, prolonged applause (7)
Escort; a group (as of vehicles) traveling together for convenience (6)
Extremely tense or nervous (7)
Ferocious; unpleasantly severe (7)
Focus one's attention on (usually a thought) for an extended period of time (5)
Give up a right or claim voluntarily (5)
In a way that is boldly rude or disrespectful (10)
Legally obligated or responsible (6)
Light, teasing, playful remarks (6)
Main enemy (9)
Mocking, taunting, or verbally abusing (7)
On the edge; the point where an action is likely to begin (5)
One leg on either side of; straddling (7)
Practice session or informal game (9)
Public performance or display (9)
Quickly (7)
Quiet; repressed; controlled (7)
Refuses to give up or let go; long-lasting (10)
Rise up or swell; bulge; lift (5)
Ruined or decayed from age, wear, or neglect (11)
Separated or moved something with great difficulty (5)
Seriously; gravely; in a somber manner (8)
Signal used to prompt an action (3)
Soaking thoroughly and completely (10)
Something or someone used to lure or mislead another into a trap (5)
Stiff; inflexible; hard (5)
Strong, vindictive, or fierce anger (5)
Surrender or give up as punishment for a crime, error, or offense (7)
Suspend (as a meeting) to or until another place or time (7)
The condition of being immediately noticeable or recognizable (10)
Threatening or dangerous (8)
Turned or swerved off course (6)
Twist into a strange shape or expression (7)
Uncommonly or infrequently found or seen (6)
Upset or disturbed (8)
Very happy or proud; in high spirits (6)
Very small, biting fly (4)
With great concentration or eager attention (8)
Written statements made under oath (10)

Tangerine Vocabulary Word Search 3

```
U D E T A R E P O O C E Y J E E R I N G
N L C F F O D Q J P V O R L R I Y V D R
P R N U F B I K L I V E J P G P F E R N
R E E M I L R Y A N L Y G I T E I R E K
E L R I D I T W O E L N D T S R L G S V
C U E G A G S C N T I J N E P I L E E N
E C V A V E A T N Z R E V C S M U X M S
D T E T I D L E I T T O Z N V E N P B Q
E A R E T E T N O S I N U E G T L L L C
N N P D S N O L I T A L S N K E L O A Y
T T M S I G W S I R M D D I C R E I N V
E L L F A H N N R A X J J M H E W T C K
D Y L S U O N I M O B R O O D E D S E J
E C F Y C U H Y M L U R R U E Y U D T
G O M N S L D L H X S T E P T R I O E V
N N I E U I K T M H I A H A Q B N I C L
I S M C B S M N F C G H T A R W F C O R
S T P L D H J E U V O I O U Q O R I Y E
T I A I U D I L N S G N Y V R X A V L K
O T T P E B T O H A C L T L A A C A V X
Y U I S D U T S E U C A E O N T T A N G
R T E E R G E N A B X I R X R E I I B M
L E N E P X R I V C T K N C D T O O N K
H S T H J N Y V E E R E D G E D N J N G
```

ADJOURN
AFFIDAVITS
AGITATED
AGONIZING
ASTRIDE
BROODED
CONSTITUTES
CONTORT
CONVOY
COOPERATED
CUE
DECOY
DWELL
ECLIPSE
ELATED
EXPLOITS
FORFEIT
FUMIGATED
GHOULISH

GNAT
HEAVE
HORTICULTURE
IMPATIENT
INCONSISTENT
INFRACTION
INSOLENTLY
INTENTLY
JEERING
JITTERY
LIABLE
MENACING
NULLIFY
OBLIGED
OMINOUSLY
OVATION
PERIMETER
PRIED
PROMINENCE

RELENTLESSLY
RELUCTANTLY
RESEMBLANCE
REVERENCE
RIGID
ROUT
SATURATING
SCARCE
SINGED
SUBDUED
TROUNCED
UNISON
UNPRECEDENTED
VEERED
VERGE
VICIOUS
WAIVE
WRATH

Tangerine Vocabulary Word Search 3 Answer Key

ADJOURN	GNAT	RELENTLESSLY
AFFIDAVITS	HEAVE	RELUCTANTLY
AGITATED	HORTICULTURE	RESEMBLANCE
AGONIZING	IMPATIENT	REVERENCE
ASTRIDE	INCONSISTENT	RIGID
BROODED	INFRACTION	ROUT
CONSTITUTES	INSOLENTLY	SATURATING
CONTORT	INTENTLY	SCARCE
CONVOY	JEERING	SINGED
COOPERATED	JITTERY	SUBDUED
CUE	LIABLE	TROUNCED
DECOY	MENACING	UNISON
DWELL	NULLIFY	UNPRECEDENTED
ECLIPSE	OBLIGED	VEERED
ELATED	OMINOUSLY	VERGE
EXPLOITS	OVATION	VICIOUS
FORFEIT	PERIMETER	WAIVE
FUMIGATED	PRIED	WRATH
GHOULISH	PROMINENCE	

Tangerine Vocabulary Word Search 4

```
A D J O U R N V E E R E D I R T S A D Y
G G W E C L I P S E L E T I C E H T G I W
J N R Q X F N Y T B S T L O T M R I S N
L I A B L E O E A I G G A O A R O T C F
W T T T F V M R P D L S P P L E U A L R
H A H G N I E S F P M P I E I L N T O S
Q R L O R N E D R E R D D R A E C E S G
X U C E L D I O A I I L A A T N E D U Q
M T P U N G M K E B R T T T E T D E R N
S A V C I I G D W D R F E E K L R D E Y
C S V R N N H N Y Q F U D D S E E O L Z
A C G E V E O E K W S C P O V S C O M B
R Q N I I X U H R P W Q M T B S E R Q X
C C I N C P L E E X B D V G L L D B E M
E N T F I L I R S O L E M N L Y I C J J
C F L R O O S P B M R T X J L M N G E P
O V E A U I H M S G N A Z T C E G D E X
N R P C S T A O E U C L N C R N S W R D
T E G T W S S C L W B E Z E M E I E I Z
O T E I H A T L Z H M D V T Y H N L N G
R N R O U T I L V E X E U O J C G L G Q
T A Z N T F L V H A R W C E X R E S D F
Y B B K Y W Y E E V P E Z B D A D V S Z
U N I S O N V J D E D S C R I M M A G E
```

ABRUPTLY
ADJOURN
AGITATED
ARCHENEMY
ASTRIDE
BANTER
BROODED
COMPREHEND
CONTORT
CONVOY
COOPERATED
CUE
DECOY
DESPISED
DILAPIDATED
DISCLOSURE
DWELL
ECLIPSE
ELATED

EXPLOITS
FORFEIT
GHOULISH
GNAT
HASTILY
HEAVE
INFRACTION
JEERING
LIABLE
NULLIFY
OBLIGED
PELTING
PERIMETER
PERSISTENT
PRIED
PROMINENCE
RECEDING
RELENTLESSLY
RETALIATE

REVERENCE
RIGID
ROUT
SATURATING
SCARCE
SCRIMMAGE
SINGED
SOLEMNLY
SUBDUED
TROUNCED
UNISON
VEERED
VEHEMENTLY
VERGE
VICIOUS
VULNERABLE
WAIVE
WRATH

Tangerine Vocabulary Word Search 4 Answer Key

```
A  D  J  O  U  R  N  V  E  E  R  E  D  I  R  T  S  A  D
G  G  W  E  C  L  I  P  S  E  L  E  I  C  E  T  G  I
   N  R        F     Y  T  B     S     L  O     R  I  S
L  I  A  B  L  E  O  E  A  I           A  O  A  R  O  T  C
   T  T  T     V  M  R  P              P  P  L  E  U  A  L
   A  H     N  I  E  S  F  P        P  I  E  I  N  C  T  O
   R        O  R  N  E  D  R  E  R     D  R  A  E  C  E  S
   U     C  E  L  D  I  O  A  I  I     A  A  T  N  E  D  U
   T     P  U     G  M  E  B        T  T  T  E  L  D  E  R
S  A  V     I     I     D     R        E  E     R  R  D  E
C  S        R  N     H  N              D        E  C  O
A     G     E  V  E  O  E              P  O     S  E  O
R     N        I  X  U  H     P           T  B  S  E  R
C  C  I     N  C  P  L  E  E        D  V     L  L  D  B  E
E     T     F  I  L  I  R  S  O  L  E  M  N  L  Y     C  J
C     L     R  O  O  S     P     R  T        L  M  N  G  E
O     E     A  U  I  H  M  S  G  N  A     T     E  G  D  E
N  R  P     C  S  T  A  O  E  U  C  L  N     R  N  S  W  R  D
T  E  T     T  W  S  S  C  L     B  E        E  E  I  E  I
O  T        I     A  T  L     H  M  D  V     Y  H  N  L  N
R  N  R     O  U  T  I        E  E  U  O        C  G  L  G
T  A        N     F        L  V  H  A  R     C  E  R  E
   B           Y        Y  E  E  V     E     D  A  D
U  N  I  S  O  N  V              E  D  S  C  R  I  M  M  A  G  E
```

ABRUPTLY	EXPLOITS	REVERENCE
ADJOURN	FORFEIT	RIGID
AGITATED	GHOULISH	ROUT
ARCHENEMY	GNAT	SATURATING
ASTRIDE	HASTILY	SCARCE
BANTER	HEAVE	SCRIMMAGE
BROODED	INFRACTION	SINGED
COMPREHEND	JEERING	SOLEMNLY
CONTORT	LIABLE	SUBDUED
CONVOY	NULLIFY	TROUNCED
COOPERATED	OBLIGED	UNISON
CUE	PELTING	VEERED
DECOY	PERIMETER	VEHEMENTLY
DESPISED	PERSISTENT	VERGE
DILAPIDATED	PRIED	VICIOUS
DISCLOSURE	PROMINENCE	VULNERABLE
DWELL	RECEDING	WAIVE
ECLIPSE	RELENTLESSLY	WRATH
ELATED	RETALIATE	

Tangerine Vocabulary Crossword 1

Across
4. Making facts and details evident and clear
6. Ferocious; unpleasantly severe
8. An overwhelming defeat
9. Escort; a group (as of vehicles) traveling together for convenience
10. Something or someone used to lure or mislead another into a trap
11. Bombarding; striking rapidly and repeatedly
14. Suspend (as a meeting) to or until another place or time
17. Subjected to smoke or fumes, usually to exterminate bugs
19. Stiff; inflexible; hard

Down
1. Very happy or proud; in high spirits
2. One leg on either side of; straddling
3. Beat severely
4. Amazement or astonishment
5. Uncommonly or infrequently found or seen
7. Makes the elements or parts of
9. Signal used to prompt an action
11. Border or boundary
12. Declare something void; invalidate
13. Upset or disturbed
14. A swell, almost like a bubble, in an artery; if it bursts, it is usually fatal
15. Required; bonded
16. Quickly
18. Corresponding exactly and occurring at the same time

Tangerine Vocabulary Crossword 1 Answer Key

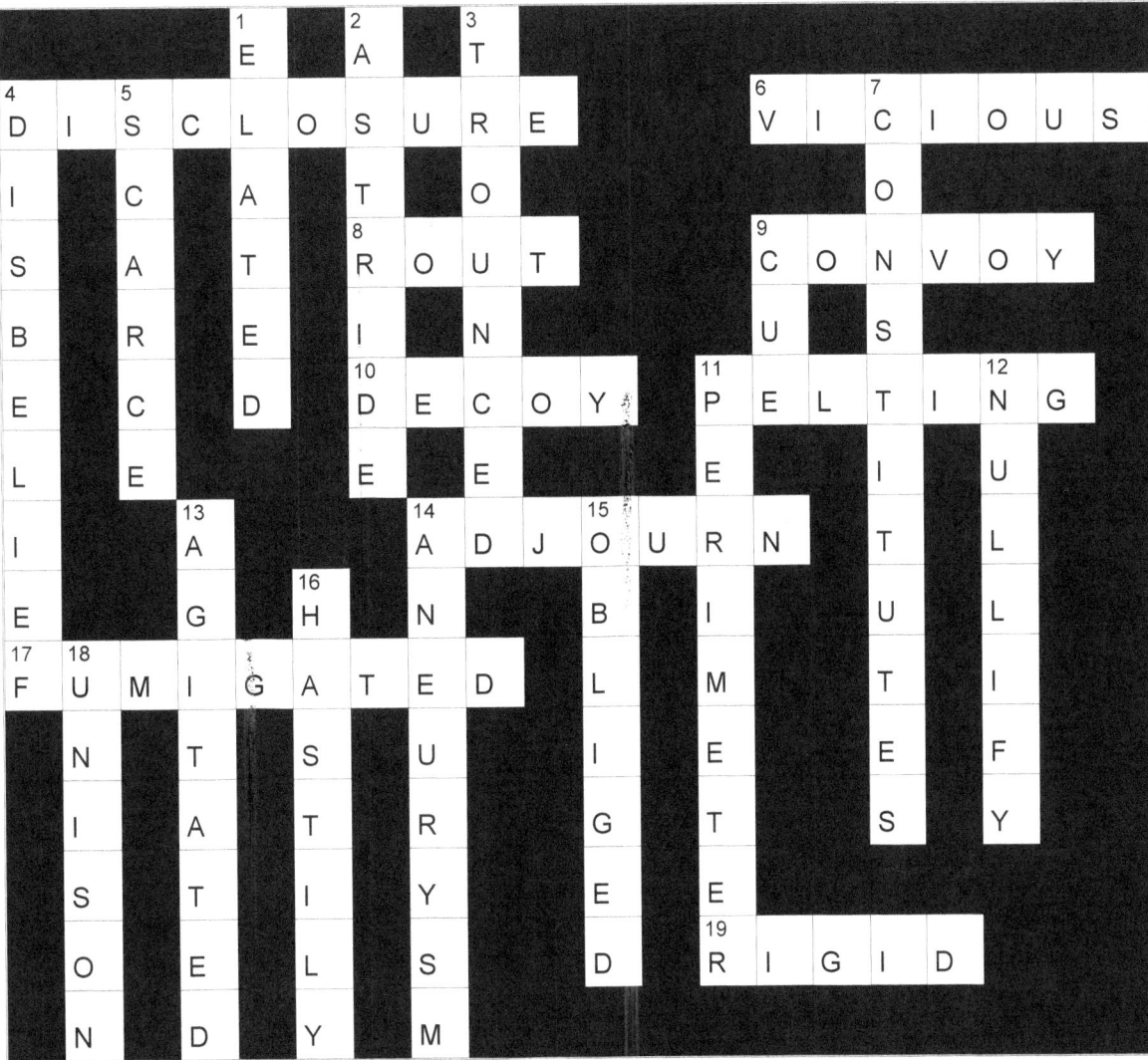

Across
4. Making facts and details evident and clear
6. Ferocious; unpleasantly severe
8. An overwhelming defeat
9. Escort; a group (as of vehicles) traveling together for convenience
10. Something or someone used to lure or mislead another into a trap
11. Bombarding; striking rapidly and repeatedly
14. Suspend (as a meeting) to or until another place or time
17. Subjected to smoke or fumes, usually to exterminate bugs
19. Stiff; inflexible; hard

Down
1. Very happy or proud; in high spirits
2. One leg on either side of; straddling
3. Beat severely
4. Amazement or astonishment
5. Uncommonly or infrequently found or seen
7. Makes the elements or parts of
9. Signal used to prompt an action
11. Border or boundary
12. Declare something void; invalidate
13. Upset or disturbed
14. A swell, almost like a bubble, in an artery; if it bursts, it is usually fatal
15. Required; bonded
16. Quickly
18. Corresponding exactly and occurring at the same time

Tangerine Vocabulary Crossword 2

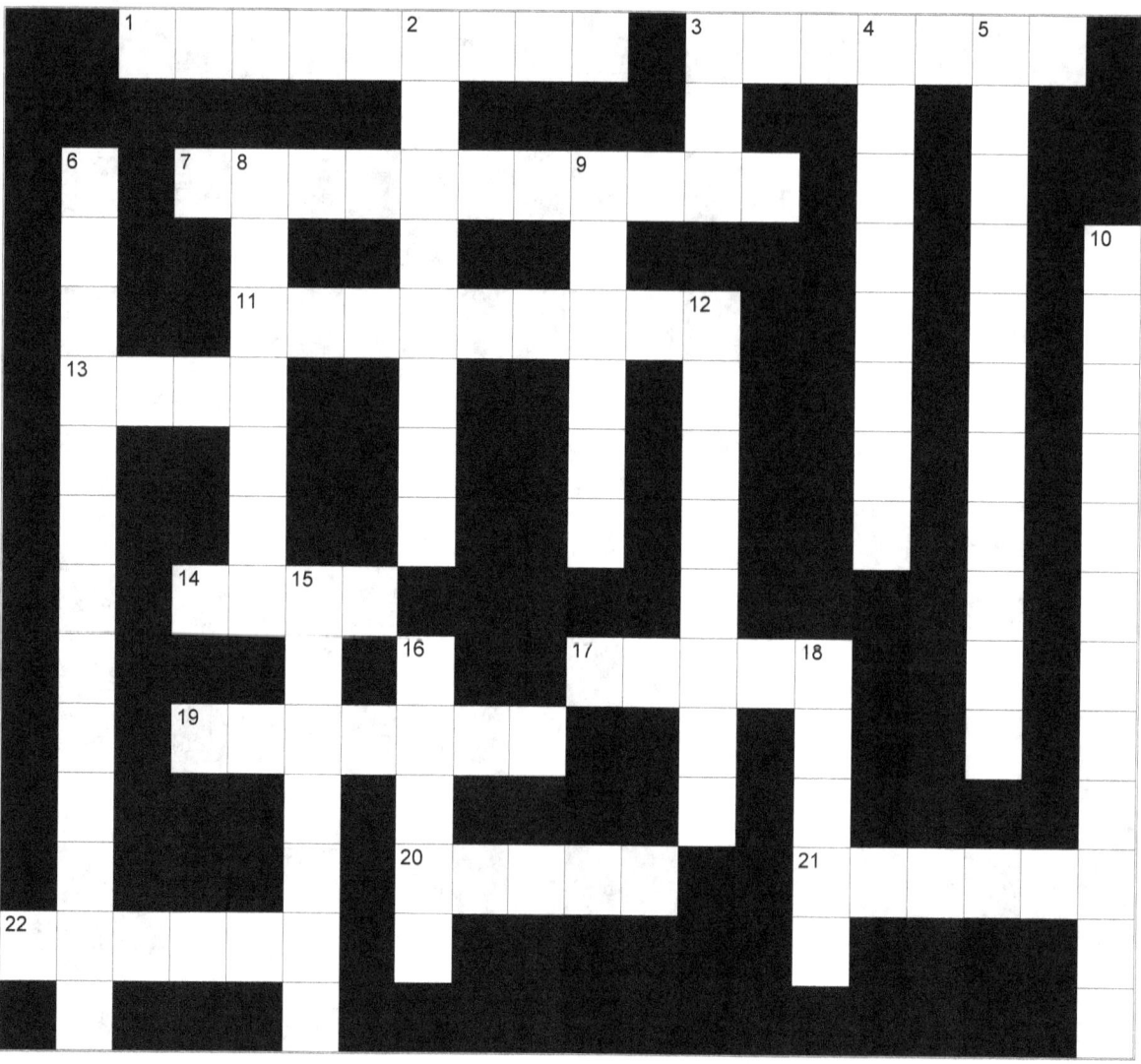

Across
1. Get revenge; pay back in kind for a wrong-doing
3. Twist into a strange shape or expression
7. Makes the elements or parts of
11. Filled with distress, suffering, or torture; worrying in a distressed way
13. An overwhelming defeat
14. Very small, biting fly
17. Separated or moved something with great difficulty
19. Extremely tense or nervous
20. On the edge; the point where an action is likely to begin
21. Legally obligated or responsible
22. Turned or swerved off course

Down
2. With great concentration or eager attention
3. Signal used to prompt an action
4. Beat severely
5. Not willingly; with resistance or hesitation
6. Never before known, experienced, or done
8. Enthusiastic, prolonged applause
9. Corresponding exactly and occurring at the same time
10. Not regular or predictable
12. Strangely cruel or monstrous
15. One leg on either side of; straddling
16. Rise up or swell; bulge; lift
18. Focus one's attention on (usually a thought) for an extended period of time

Tangerine Vocabulary Crossword 2 Answer Key

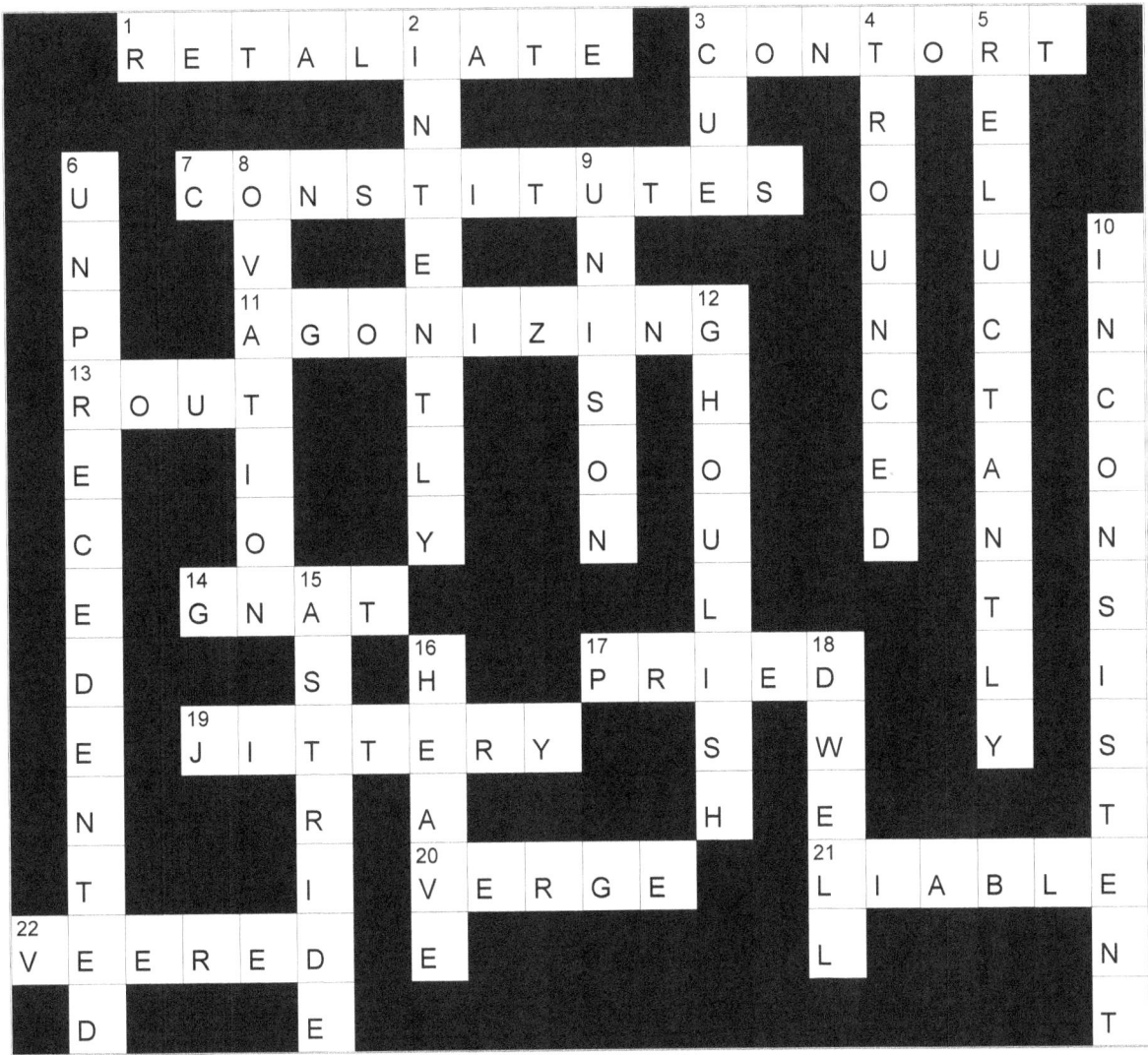

Across
1. Get revenge; pay back in kind for a wrong-doing
3. Twist into a strange shape or expression
7. Makes the elements or parts of
11. Filled with distress, suffering, or torture; worrying in a distressed way
13. An overwhelming defeat
14. Very small, biting fly
17. Separated or moved something with great difficulty
19. Extremely tense or nervous
20. On the edge; the point where an action is likely to begin
21. Legally obligated or responsible
22. Turned or swerved off course

Down
2. With great concentration or eager attention
3. Signal used to prompt an action
4. Beat severely
5. Not willingly; with resistance or hesitation
6. Never before known, experienced, or done
8. Enthusiastic, prolonged applause
9. Corresponding exactly and occurring at the same time
10. Not regular or predictable
12. Strangely cruel or monstrous
15. One leg on either side of; straddling
16. Rise up or swell; bulge; lift
18. Focus one's attention on (usually a thought) for an extended period of time

Tangerine Vocabulary Crossword 3

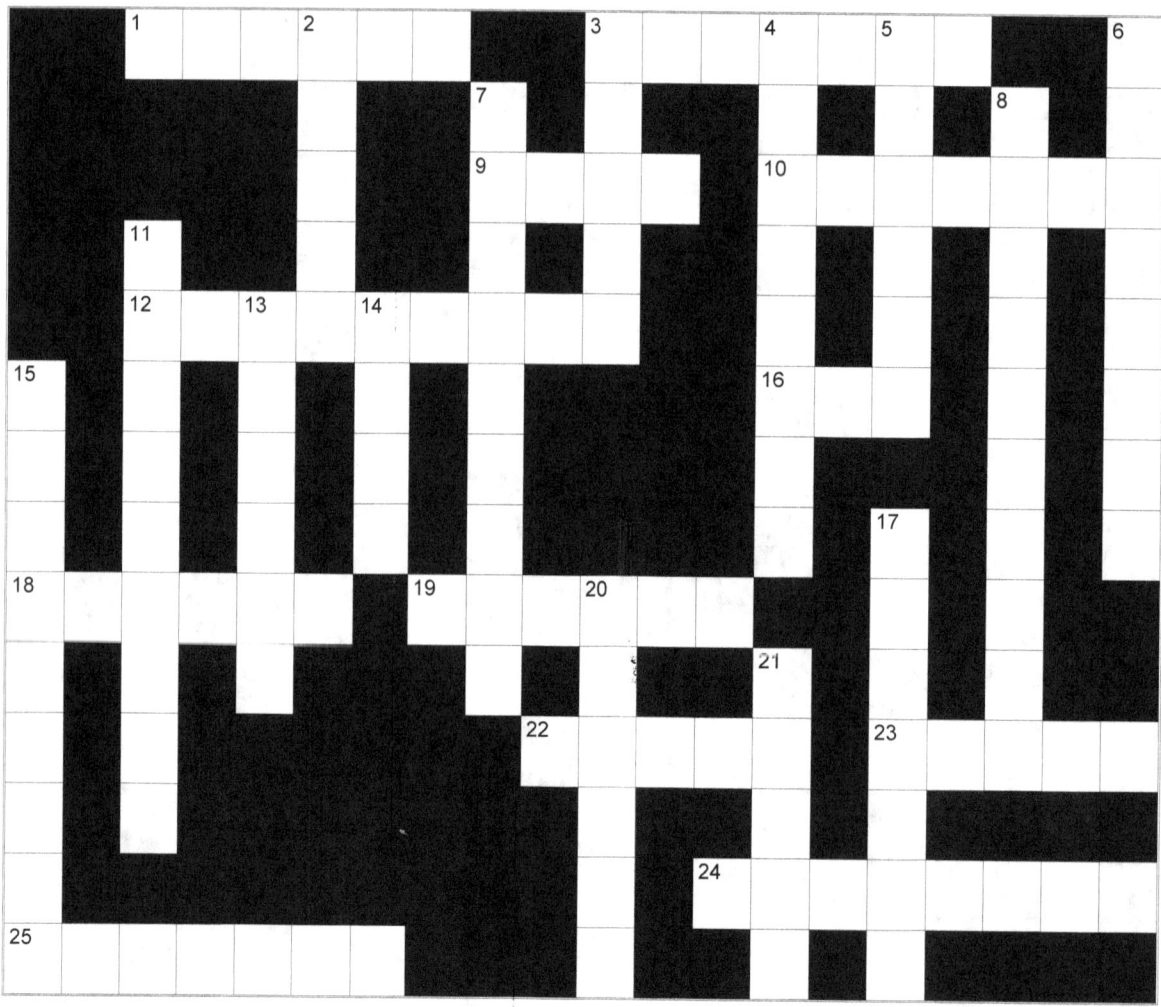

Across
1. Escort; a group (as of vehicles) traveling together for convenience
3. Quickly
9. Very small, biting fly
10. Enthusiastic, prolonged applause
12. Feeling or attitude of deep respect
16. Signal used to prompt an action
18. Light, teasing, playful remarks
19. Corresponding exactly and occurring at the same time
22. Give up a right or claim voluntarily
23. Focus one's attention on (usually a thought) for an extended period of time
24. Seriously; gravely; in a somber manner
25. Surrender or give up as punishment for a crime, error, or offense

Down
2. On the edge; the point where an action is likely to begin
3. Rise up or swell; bulge; lift
4. Beat severely
5. Legally obligated or responsible
6. Threatening or dangerous
7. Filled with distress, suffering, or torture; worrying in a distressed way
8. Making facts and details evident and clear
11. Main enemy
13. Turned or swerved off course
14. An overwhelming defeat
15. Amazement or astonishment
17. Quiet; repressed; controlled
20. Uncommonly or infrequently found or seen
21. Something or someone used to lure or mislead another into a trap

Tangerine Vocabulary Crossword 3 Answer Key

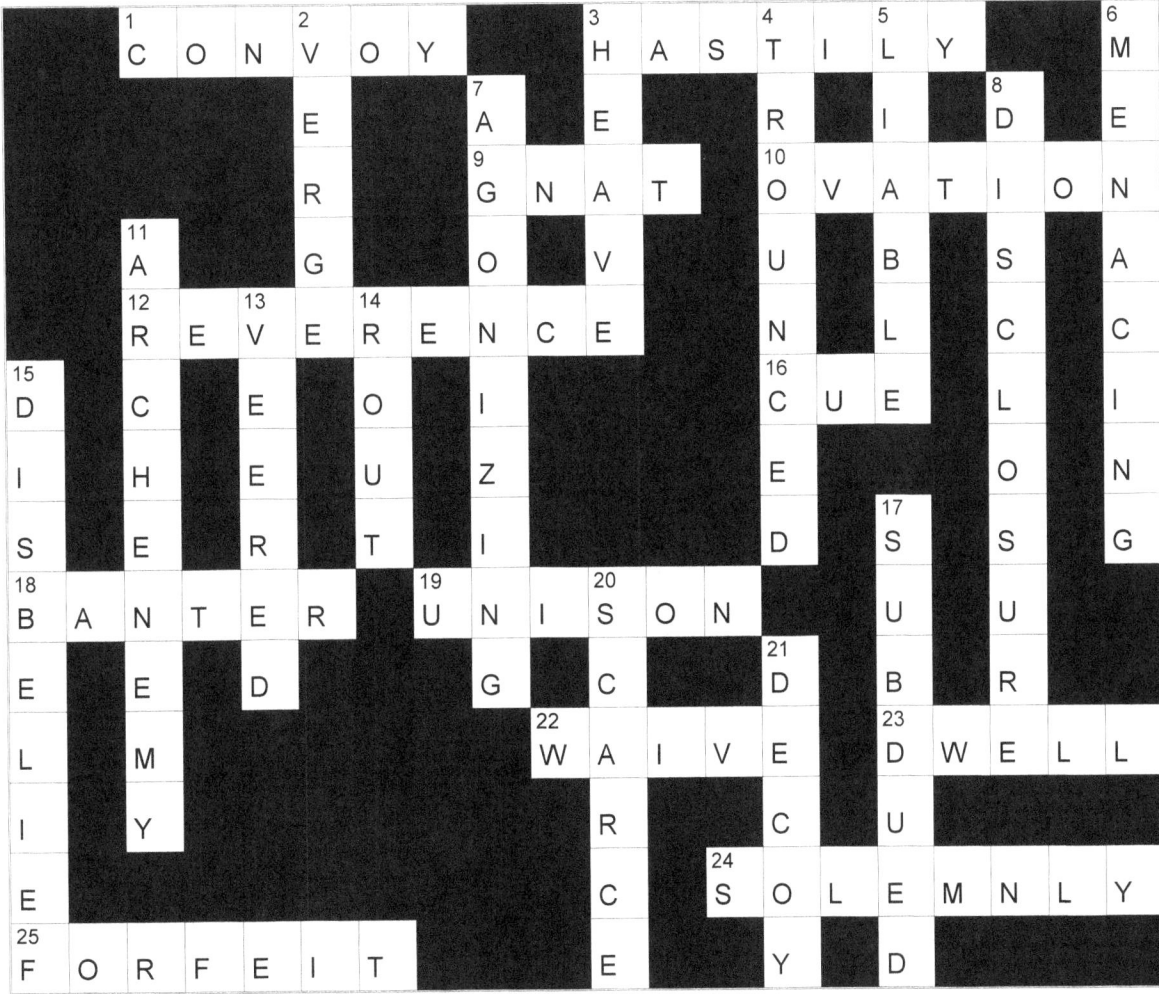

Across
1. Escort; a group (as of vehicles) traveling together for convenience
3. Quickly
9. Very small, biting fly
10. Enthusiastic, prolonged applause
12. Feeling or attitude of deep respect
16. Signal used to prompt an action
18. Light, teasing, playful remarks
19. Corresponding exactly and occurring at the same time
22. Give up a right or claim voluntarily
23. Focus one's attention on (usually a thought) for an extended period of time
24. Seriously; gravely; in a somber manner
25. Surrender or give up as punishment for a crime, error, or offense

Down
2. On the edge; the point where an action is likely to begin
3. Rise up or swell; bulge; lift
4. Beat severely
5. Legally obligated or responsible
6. Threatening or dangerous
7. Filled with distress, suffering, or torture; worrying in a distressed way
8. Making facts and details evident and clear
11. Main enemy
13. Turned or swerved off course
14. An overwhelming defeat
15. Amazement or astonishment
17. Quiet; repressed; controlled
20. Uncommonly or infrequently found or seen
21. Something or someone used to lure or mislead another into a trap

Tangerine Vocabulary Crossword 4

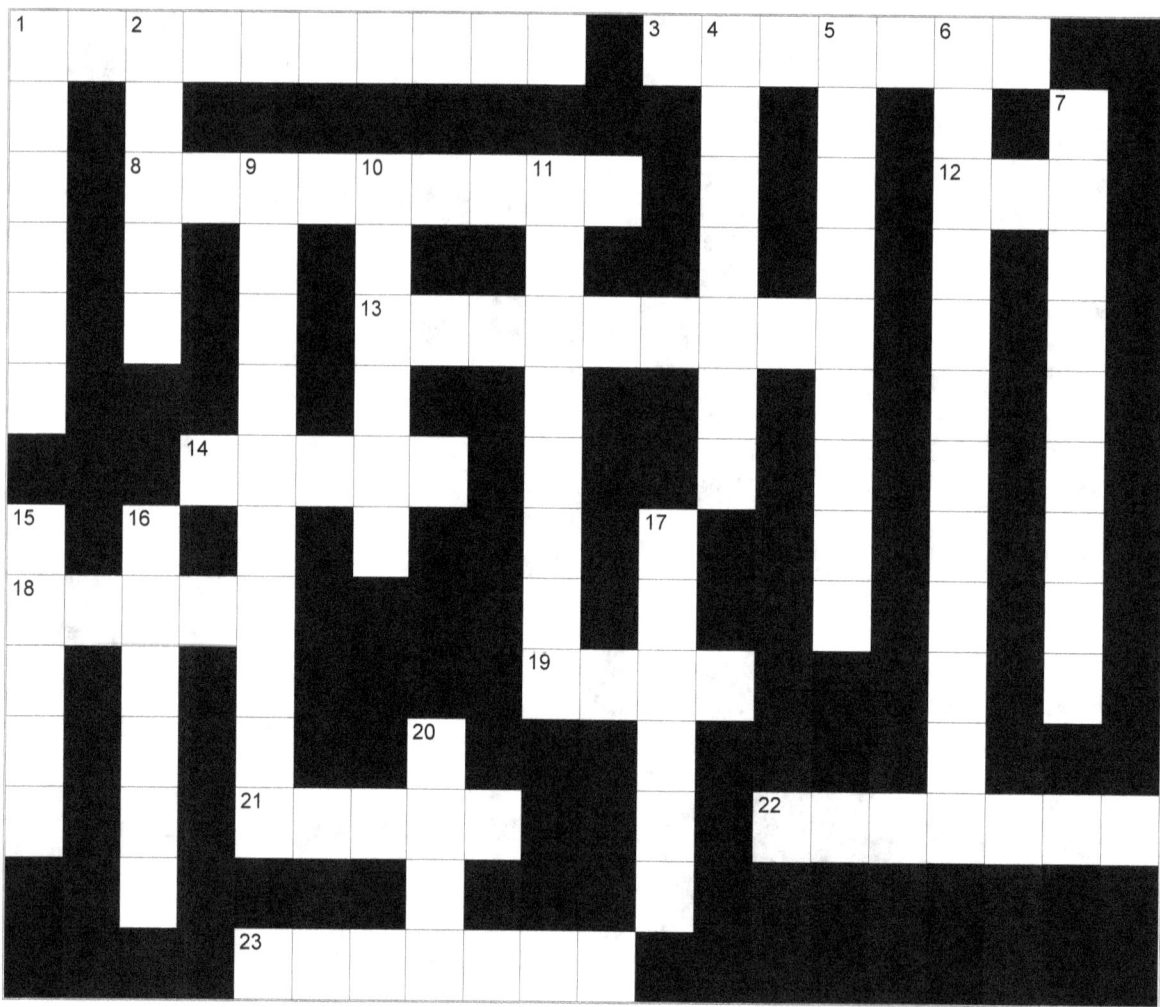

Across
1. Strongly; violently; with forceful expression of emotion or belief
3. Surrender or give up as punishment for a crime, error, or offense
8. Main enemy
12. Signal used to prompt an action
13. Filled with distress, suffering, or torture; worrying in a distressed way
14. Separated or moved something with great difficulty
18. Strong, vindictive, or fierce anger
19. Very small, biting fly
21. Something or someone used to lure or mislead another into a trap
22. Quickly
23. Twist into a strange shape or expression

Down
1. Turned or swerved off course
2. Rise up or swell; bulge; lift
4. Enthusiastic, prolonged applause
5. Subjected to smoke or fumes, usually to exterminate bugs
6. Not regular or predictable
7. Border or boundary
9. Understand
10. Very happy or proud; in high spirits
11. Threatening or dangerous
15. Focus one's attention on (usually a thought) for an extended period of time
16. Light, teasing, playful remarks
17. Legally obligated or responsible
20. An overwhelming defeat

Tangerine Vocabulary Crossword 4 Answer Key

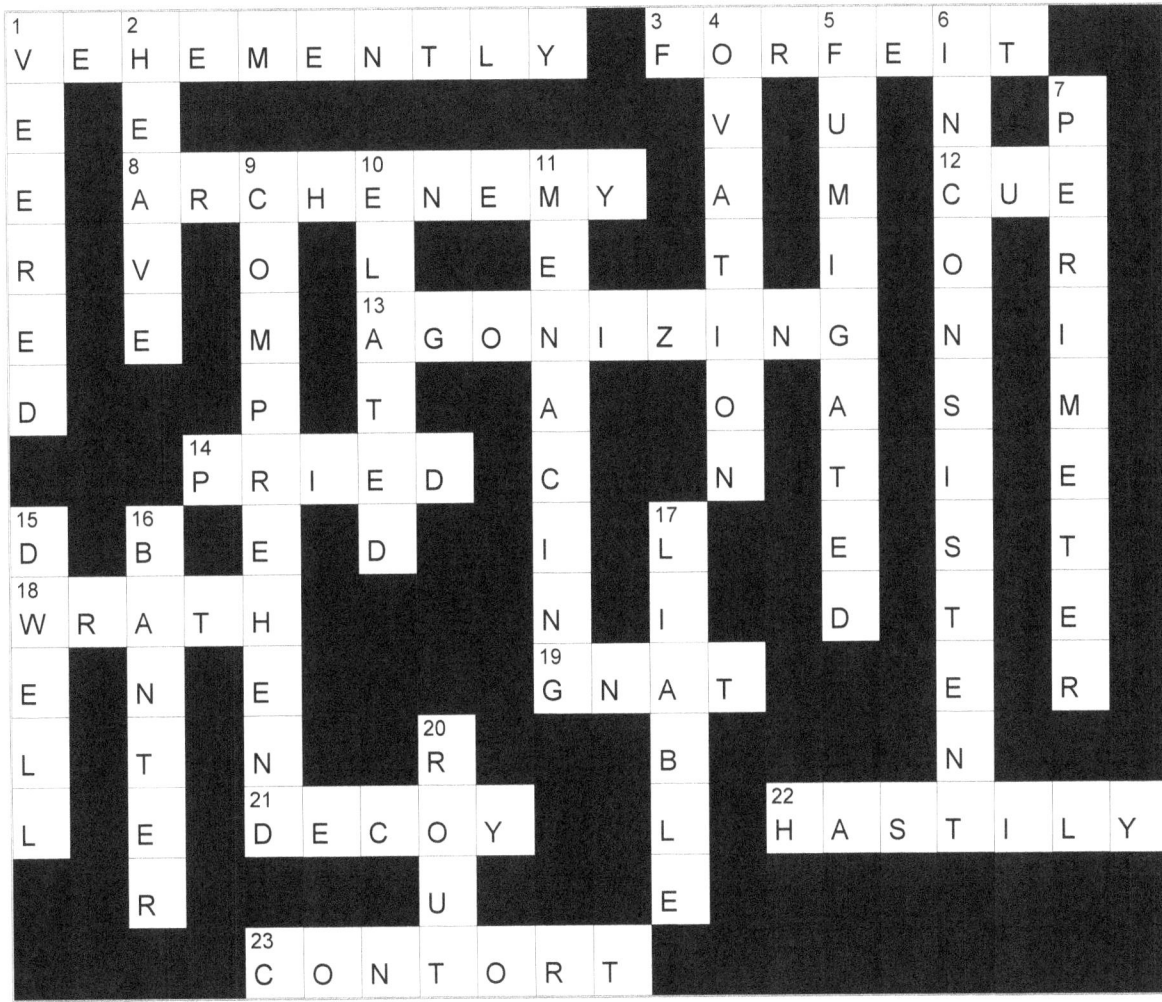

Across
1. Strongly; violently; with forceful expression of emotion or belief
3. Surrender or give up as punishment for a crime, error, or offense
8. Main enemy
12. Signal used to prompt an action
13. Filled with distress, suffering, or torture; worrying in a distressed way
14. Separated or moved something with great difficulty
18. Strong, vindictive, or fierce anger
19. Very small, biting fly
21. Something or someone used to lure or mislead another into a trap
22. Quickly
23. Twist into a strange shape or expression

Down
1. Turned or swerved off course
2. Rise up or swell; bulge; lift
4. Enthusiastic, prolonged applause
5. Subjected to smoke or fumes, usually to exterminate bugs
6. Not regular or predictable
7. Border or boundary
9. Understand
10. Very happy or proud; in high spirits
11. Threatening or dangerous
15. Focus one's attention on (usually a thought) for an extended period of time
16. Light, teasing, playful remarks
17. Legally obligated or responsible
20. An overwhelming defeat

ABRUPTLY	Suddenly or unexpectedly
ADJOURN	Suspend (as a meeting) to or until another place or time
AFFIDAVITS	Written statements made under oath
AGITATED	Upset or disturbed
AGONIZING	Filled with distress, suffering, or torture; worrying in a distressed way

ANEURYSM	A swell, almost like a bubble, in an artery; if it bursts, it is usually fatal
ARCHENEMY	Main enemy
ASTRIDE	One leg on either side of; straddling
BANTER	Light, teasing, playful remarks
BILLOWING	Moving (usually upward or outward) in a rolling, swelling motion

BROODED	Was in deep thought; focused attention on one subject persistently
CALISTHENICS	Exercises to develop muscles
CAPSIZING	Turning or flipping over
COMPREHEND	Understand
CONSCIENCE	One's own moral or ethical awareness of right and wrong

CONSTITUTES	Makes the elements or parts of
CONTORT	Twist into a strange shape or expression
CONVICTION	Fixed or firm belief
CONVOY	Escort; a group (as of vehicles) traveling together for convenience
COOPERATED	Worked together willingly and agreeably

CORRUGATED	Having folds, ridges, and grooves
CUE	Signal used to prompt an action
DECOY	Something or someone used to lure or mislead another into a trap
DESPISED	Disliked intensely; scorned; loathed
DILAPIDATED	Ruined or decayed from age, wear, or neglect

DISBELIEF	Amazement or astonishment
DISCLOSURE	Making facts and details evident and clear
DISINFECTANT	Chemical agent used to destroy bacteria
DISINTEGRATING	Breaking up; deteriorating; falling apart
DWELL	Focus one's attention on (usually a thought) for an extended period of time

ECLIPSE	The disappearance of the whole or a part of the sun when the moon comes between it and earth
ELATED	Very happy or proud; in high spirits
EXPLOITS	Outstanding events in which a person puts his or her strong points to the best advantage
FORFEIT	Surrender or give up as punishment for a crime, error, or offense
FUMIGATED	Subjected to smoke or fumes, usually to exterminate bugs

GHOULISH	Strangely cruel or monstrous
GNAT	Very small, biting fly
HASTILY	Quickly
HEAVE	Rise up or swell; bulge; lift
HORTICULTURE	The science or art of cultivating plants

IMPATIENT	Wanting to hurry up; not wanting to wait for something to be done or to happen
INCONSISTENT	Not regular or predictable
INFRACTION	Violation; breach
INSOLENTLY	In a way that is boldly rude or disrespectful
INTENTLY	With great concentration or eager attention

INTERVENED	Came between to mediate or help
IRREGULARITIES	Things that are not within the usual rules or customs
JEERING	Mocking, taunting, or verbally abusing
JITTERY	Extremely tense or nervous
LIABLE	Legally obligated or responsible

MENACING	Threatening or dangerous
NULLIFY	Declare something void; invalidate
OBLIGED	Required; bonded
OMINOUSLY	In a threatening way
OVATION	Enthusiastic, prolonged applause

PARALLEL	Extending in the same direction, equally distant at every point
PELTING	Bombarding; striking rapidly and repeatedly
PERIMETER	Border or boundary
PERSISTENT	Refuses to give up or let go; long-lasting
PRIED	Separated or moved something with great difficulty

PROMINENCE	The condition of being immediately noticeable or recognizable
PROSTRATE	Lying flat on the ground in humility or submission
RECEDING	Becoming more distant
RELENTLESSLY	Steadily; in a way never giving up
RELUCTANTLY	Not willingly; with resistance or hesitation

RESEMBLANCE	Similarity of likeness with something else
RESTITUTION	Compensation for loss or damage
RETALIATE	Get revenge; pay back in kind for a wrong-doing
REVERENCE	Feeling or attitude of deep respect
RIGID	Stiff; inflexible; hard

ROUT	An overwhelming defeat
SATURATING	Soaking thoroughly and completely
SCARCE	Uncommonly or infrequently found or seen
SCRIMMAGE	Practice session or informal game
SINGED	Burned slightly; scorched

SOLEMNLY	Seriously; gravely; in a somber manner
SPECTACLE	Public performance or display
SUBDUED	Quiet; repressed; controlled
TROUNCED	Beat severely
UNISON	Corresponding exactly and occurring at the same time

UNPRECEDENTED	Never before known, experienced, or done
VEERED	Turned or swerved off course
VEHEMENTLY	Strongly; violently; with forceful expression of emotion or belief
VERGE	On the edge; the point where an action is likely to begin
VICIOUS	Ferocious; unpleasantly severe

VULNERABLE	Capable of being wounded or hurt
WAIVE	Give up a right or claim voluntarily
WRATH	Strong, vindictive, or fierce anger

Tangerine Vocabulary

ADJOURN	UNISON	LIABLE	VEHEMENTLY	SATURATING
OMINOUSLY	INTENTLY	SUBDUED	CALISTHENICS	ASTRIDE
IMPATIENT	EXPLOITS	FREE SPACE	DESPISED	INFRACTION
CORRUGATED	COOPERATED	VICIOUS	SOLEMNLY	INSOLENTLY
PERIMETER	COMPREHEND	RECEDING	DISBELIEF	JEERING

Tangerine Vocabulary

AGONIZING	RESEMBLANCE	VERGE	RELUCTANTLY	ROUT
ANEURYSM	JITTERY	DECOY	CONVICTION	REVERENCE
PRIED	CUE	FREE SPACE	HORTICULTURE	PELTING
SCRIMMAGE	RELENTLESSLY	CONVOY	GNAT	PARALLEL
OVATION	CONTORT	AFFIDAVITS	ELATED	TROUNCED

Tangerine Vocabulary

OMINOUSLY	GNAT	JITTERY	INCONSISTENT	DILAPIDATED
FUMIGATED	RELENTLESSLY	DISCLOSURE	LIABLE	OVATION
HASTILY	COOPERATED	FREE SPACE	PROSTRATE	GHOULISH
BROODED	SCARCE	INSOLENTLY	PARALLEL	BANTER
CONSCIENCE	MENACING	PERIMETER	AGONIZING	DISINTEGRATING

Tangerine Vocabulary

VULNERABLE	DESPISED	SINGED	IRREGULARITIES	UNISON
WAIVE	EXPLOITS	CONVICTION	SUBDUED	ASTRIDE
RESTITUTION	REVERENCE	FREE SPACE	AFFIDAVITS	RELUCTANTLY
SPECTACLE	HEAVE	NULLIFY	BILLOWING	INTENTLY
JEERING	COMPREHEND	SATURATING	CONVOY	VERGE

Tangerine Vocabulary

INCONSISTENT	SUBDUED	HEAVE	CONSCIENCE	RELENTLESSLY
HASTILY	ABRUPTLY	PELTING	CORRUGATED	CONSTITUTES
OBLIGED	VERGE	FREE SPACE	AGONIZING	AFFIDAVITS
RESEMBLANCE	WAIVE	CALISTHENICS	ELATED	DILAPIDATED
SOLEMNLY	MENACING	OVATION	TROUNCED	INTERVENED

Tangerine Vocabulary

PARALLEL	VICIOUS	UNISON	PERIMETER	PROSTRATE
DWELL	LIABLE	NULLIFY	ASTRIDE	SCARCE
RETALIATE	BROODED	FREE SPACE	COOPERATED	DISCLOSURE
DECOY	ARCHENEMY	COMPREHEND	DISINTEGRATING	SINGED
VEERED	AGITATED	SATURATING	CUE	RECEDING

Tangerine Vocabulary

BILLOWING	CUE	ROUT	PRIED	AFFIDAVITS
OMINOUSLY	DECOY	SOLEMNLY	CONVOY	IMPATIENT
FUMIGATED	AGITATED	FREE SPACE	UNISON	SPECTACLE
HEAVE	OBLIGED	IRREGULARITIES	HORTICULTURE	WRATH
PARALLEL	PELTING	RETALIATE	SCARCE	GHOULISH

Tangerine Vocabulary

PROMINENCE	ADJOURN	PROSTRATE	DISINFECTANT	ANEURYSM
ELATED	DISCLOSURE	VULNERABLE	DISBELIEF	VERGE
AGONIZING	CONSTITUTES	FREE SPACE	RELENTLESSLY	PERSISTENT
COOPERATED	RESTITUTION	SCRIMMAGE	JITTERY	SINGED
HASTILY	DESPISED	UNPRECEDENTED	INFRACTION	BANTER

Tangerine Vocabulary

ARCHENEMY	AGONIZING	VERGE	REVERENCE	FUMIGATED
INCONSISTENT	INTERVENED	PELTING	VEERED	PROSTRATE
VEHEMENTLY	ELATED	FREE SPACE	CONVICTION	TROUNCED
CORRUGATED	DISINFECTANT	GHOULISH	IMPATIENT	BILLOWING
DILAPIDATED	PROMINENCE	EXPLOITS	DESPISED	CONSTITUTES

Tangerine Vocabulary

PRIED	INSOLENTLY	JEERING	RIGID	JITTERY
FORFEIT	BANTER	GNAT	BROODED	RESTITUTION
UNPRECEDENTED	WAIVE	FREE SPACE	SPECTACLE	OMINOUSLY
AFFIDAVITS	VULNERABLE	DISCLOSURE	VICIOUS	DISBELIEF
OBLIGED	DWELL	UNISON	ECLIPSE	MENACING

Tangerine Vocabulary

DESPISED	CUE	ARCHENEMY	ROUT	DISINFECTANT
RECEDING	UNPRECEDENTED	SCRIMMAGE	RELENTLESSLY	MENACING
PROMINENCE	RESEMBLANCE	FREE SPACE	UNISON	COMPREHEND
FUMIGATED	IRREGULARITIES	GNAT	VICIOUS	SATURATING
RETALIATE	CONVICTION	ABRUPTLY	HEAVE	DWELL

Tangerine Vocabulary

ELATED	CONVOY	BANTER	VERGE	CONSCIENCE
REVERENCE	ASTRIDE	VEHEMENTLY	CORRUGATED	SPECTACLE
PRIED	DISINTEGRATING	FREE SPACE	INFRACTION	SINGED
DILAPIDATED	PERSISTENT	WAIVE	AGONIZING	RELUCTANTLY
INSOLENTLY	OMINOUSLY	RESTITUTION	ANEURYSM	CAPSIZING

Tangerine Vocabulary

SOLEMNLY	INSOLENTLY	DISINFECTANT	CUE	SUBDUED
SPECTACLE	ANEURYSM	OBLIGED	BILLOWING	RELENTLESSLY
JEERING	HEAVE	FREE SPACE	VEHEMENTLY	JITTERY
ELATED	COMPREHEND	CONTORT	ROUT	LIABLE
AGITATED	CONSTITUTES	VICIOUS	INTENTLY	ARCHENEMY

Tangerine Vocabulary

WRATH	FORFEIT	DILAPIDATED	EXPLOITS	VULNERABLE
MENACING	NULLIFY	SINGED	WAIVE	HORTICULTURE
INCONSISTENT	SCARCE	FREE SPACE	UNPRECEDENTED	INFRACTION
AGONIZING	DESPISED	RESEMBLANCE	INTERVENED	SCRIMMAGE
CAPSIZING	CONVICTION	RELUCTANTLY	PARALLEL	VERGE

Tangerine Vocabulary

OVATION	PROSTRATE	LIABLE	GNAT	DISBELIEF
REVERENCE	DISINTEGRATING	DILAPIDATED	AFFIDAVITS	SUBDUED
IRREGULARITIES	DWELL	FREE SPACE	RELUCTANTLY	NULLIFY
OBLIGED	CONTORT	FORFEIT	FUMIGATED	IMPATIENT
JITTERY	ARCHENEMY	SOLEMNLY	CORRUGATED	INSOLENTLY

Tangerine Vocabulary

RESEMBLANCE	BANTER	TROUNCED	INFRACTION	ECLIPSE
VICIOUS	UNPRECEDENTED	VEHEMENTLY	RECEDING	PRIED
WRATH	WAIVE	FREE SPACE	CALISTHENICS	AGONIZING
DECOY	INCONSISTENT	PERSISTENT	HEAVE	COMPREHEND
INTERVENED	VERGE	DISCLOSURE	JEERING	CONSTITUTES

Tangerine Vocabulary

COMPREHEND	SCRIMMAGE	CONVICTION	PARALLEL	WRATH
UNPRECEDENTED	BROODED	CONSTITUTES	GNAT	MENACING
DISINFECTANT	RELUCTANTLY	FREE SPACE	DISBELIEF	INSOLENTLY
SCARCE	PERIMETER	ROUT	BANTER	INTENTLY
VICIOUS	FORFEIT	CONTORT	INFRACTION	IRREGULARITIES

Tangerine Vocabulary

CAPSIZING	OMINOUSLY	PROMINENCE	RESEMBLANCE	REVERENCE
OVATION	AGONIZING	COOPERATED	DISINTEGRATING	SINGED
CONSCIENCE	DILAPIDATED	FREE SPACE	SOLEMNLY	DECOY
CORRUGATED	PERSISTENT	HASTILY	HORTICULTURE	ECLIPSE
TROUNCED	CUE	ANEURYSM	VULNERABLE	HEAVE

Tangerine Vocabulary

SCARCE	REVERENCE	FUMIGATED	TROUNCED	EXPLOITS
VERGE	RIGID	NULLIFY	GNAT	UNISON
HASTILY	WAIVE	FREE SPACE	IMPATIENT	SATURATING
GHOULISH	INFRACTION	OVATION	JITTERY	ABRUPTLY
RELUCTANTLY	ARCHENEMY	INTENTLY	PERIMETER	INCONSISTENT

Tangerine Vocabulary

PROMINENCE	BILLOWING	DISBELIEF	HEAVE	CONTORT
WRATH	CORRUGATED	PELTING	SCRIMMAGE	VEERED
IRREGULARITIES	AGONIZING	FREE SPACE	INTERVENED	PROSTRATE
ASTRIDE	MENACING	ANEURYSM	PERSISTENT	CONVOY
DILAPIDATED	RESEMBLANCE	CAPSIZING	BROODED	DECOY

Tangerine Vocabulary

WAIVE	VEERED	PRIED	HEAVE	PERSISTENT
IMPATIENT	SINGED	WRATH	CAPSIZING	ASTRIDE
AGITATED	DISCLOSURE	FREE SPACE	IRREGULARITIES	VERGE
LIABLE	HORTICULTURE	SPECTACLE	CORRUGATED	GNAT
SATURATING	SUBDUED	CONSCIENCE	VEHEMENTLY	BROODED

Tangerine Vocabulary

ROUT	VULNERABLE	OVATION	CUE	CALISTHENICS
INSOLENTLY	RELUCTANTLY	PERIMETER	UNISON	PELTING
CONSTITUTES	VICIOUS	FREE SPACE	AFFIDAVITS	CONTORT
PROMINENCE	FORFEIT	COOPERATED	GHOULISH	RELENTLESSLY
ARCHENEMY	DWELL	COMPREHEND	CONVOY	TROUNCED

Tangerine Vocabulary

TROUNCED	AGITATED	ANEURYSM	FORFEIT	RELUCTANTLY
CUE	PROMINENCE	CONSTITUTES	ROUT	BILLOWING
INFRACTION	ASTRIDE	FREE SPACE	PERSISTENT	JEERING
VEERED	BROODED	DESPISED	WRATH	GNAT
SOLEMNLY	RETALIATE	JITTERY	RELENTLESSLY	SINGED

Tangerine Vocabulary

RECEDING	VULNERABLE	PELTING	PROSTRATE	IMPATIENT
VERGE	CONVICTION	INCONSISTENT	CONTORT	COOPERATED
DISBELIEF	SPECTACLE	FREE SPACE	WAIVE	RIGID
RESEMBLANCE	DILAPIDATED	CONVOY	PARALLEL	UNPRECEDENTED
EXPLOITS	HORTICULTURE	DISINFECTANT	SUBDUED	SCRIMMAGE

Tangerine Vocabulary

INCONSISTENT	SCRIMMAGE	INTENTLY	VERGE	IRREGULARITIES
DISINFECTANT	BILLOWING	PERSISTENT	DILAPIDATED	CORRUGATED
OMINOUSLY	CALISTHENICS	FREE SPACE	COOPERATED	CONSCIENCE
ROUT	GHOULISH	ARCHENEMY	VEERED	FORFEIT
WAIVE	ADJOURN	RESTITUTION	RELENTLESSLY	SATURATING

Tangerine Vocabulary

FUMIGATED	PRIED	MENACING	REVERENCE	HEAVE
CONSTITUTES	UNISON	DESPISED	DISINTEGRATING	ASTRIDE
SOLEMNLY	PELTING	FREE SPACE	COMPREHEND	DWELL
DISBELIEF	GNAT	DECOY	SCARCE	PROSTRATE
CAPSIZING	SPECTACLE	OBLIGED	OVATION	WRATH

Tangerine Vocabulary

SUBDUED	RELUCTANTLY	IMPATIENT	SOLEMNLY	DISINTEGRATING
SATURATING	INCONSISTENT	JEERING	INFRACTION	PERSISTENT
DISBELIEF	RELENTLESSLY	FREE SPACE	VICIOUS	RESTITUTION
BROODED	GHOULISH	MENACING	RESEMBLANCE	UNISON
TROUNCED	DISINFECTANT	INTERVENED	WAIVE	PROSTRATE

Tangerine Vocabulary

CONSTITUTES	SINGED	CALISTHENICS	RETALIATE	VERGE
BILLOWING	PARALLEL	NULLIFY	FUMIGATED	CAPSIZING
DESPISED	DISCLOSURE	FREE SPACE	PROMINENCE	PRIED
CONVOY	RIGID	SPECTACLE	ANEURYSM	PERIMETER
ADJOURN	INSOLENTLY	OVATION	UNPRECEDENTED	ASTRIDE

Tangerine Vocabulary

CONSCIENCE	COMPREHEND	ADJOURN	JEERING	PERSISTENT
COOPERATED	NULLIFY	GHOULISH	RELENTLESSLY	SATURATING
INSOLENTLY	PROSTRATE	FREE SPACE	UNISON	CONVOY
ASTRIDE	CALISTHENICS	HEAVE	RESTITUTION	LIABLE
DILAPIDATED	VERGE	UNPRECEDENTED	CONVICTION	DISCLOSURE

Tangerine Vocabulary

VULNERABLE	SUBDUED	INCONSISTENT	AGITATED	RESEMBLANCE
SCARCE	CAPSIZING	OMINOUSLY	INTERVENED	VICIOUS
RELUCTANTLY	SCRIMMAGE	FREE SPACE	PROMINENCE	ANEURYSM
ARCHENEMY	BROODED	OBLIGED	CUE	SOLEMNLY
CORRUGATED	DECOY	INTENTLY	PRIED	IRREGULARITIES

Tangerine Vocabulary

ELATED	HASTILY	ROUT	WAIVE	EXPLOITS
SCARCE	ADJOURN	PELTING	INCONSISTENT	VEHEMENTLY
FORFEIT	IRREGULARITIES	FREE SPACE	WRATH	MENACING
CUE	RETALIATE	DILAPIDATED	SATURATING	ECLIPSE
INTENTLY	AGITATED	RIGID	VICIOUS	DISCLOSURE

Tangerine Vocabulary

RELENTLESSLY	INFRACTION	HORTICULTURE	JITTERY	SPECTACLE
BILLOWING	PERSISTENT	VEERED	SUBDUED	VERGE
NULLIFY	SINGED	FREE SPACE	COOPERATED	UNPRECEDENTED
OBLIGED	CAPSIZING	CONSCIENCE	GHOULISH	PRIED
PARALLEL	AGONIZING	JEERING	PROSTRATE	RECEDING

www.ingramcontent.com/pod-product-compliance
Lightning Source LLC
Chambersburg PA
CBHW081450070526
44586CB00019B/2291